Let these illustrations
be the starting guide to
your fun and colorful
imagination! Orange cats!
Blue dogs! Maybe even a
purple horse! Or, try for
a bit of realism!

Crayons, pastels, colored
pencils, colored pens . . .
whatever you decide!

There is no right
or wrong way! Only
your way!

Have fun! :)

– Ward

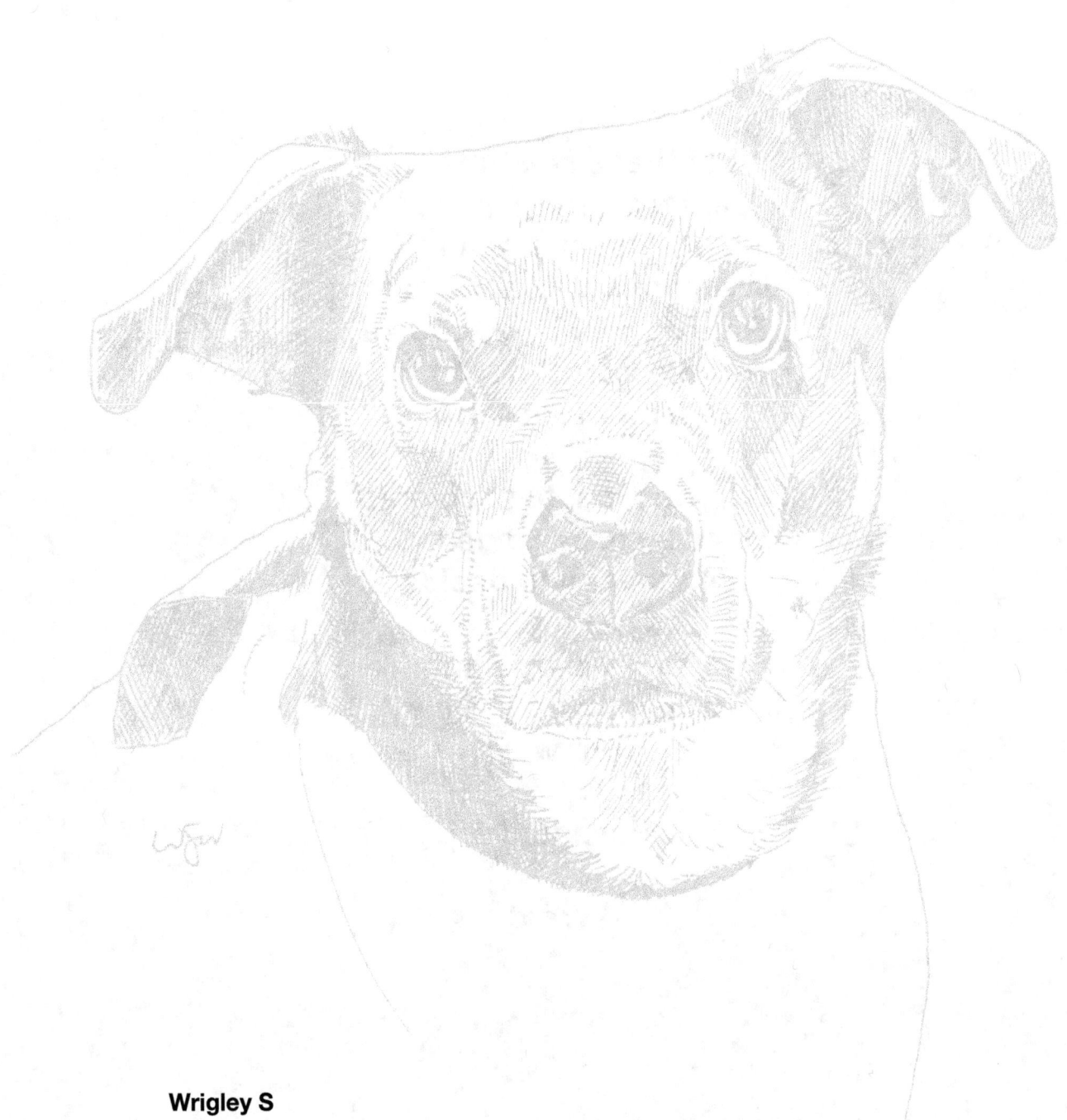

Wrigley S

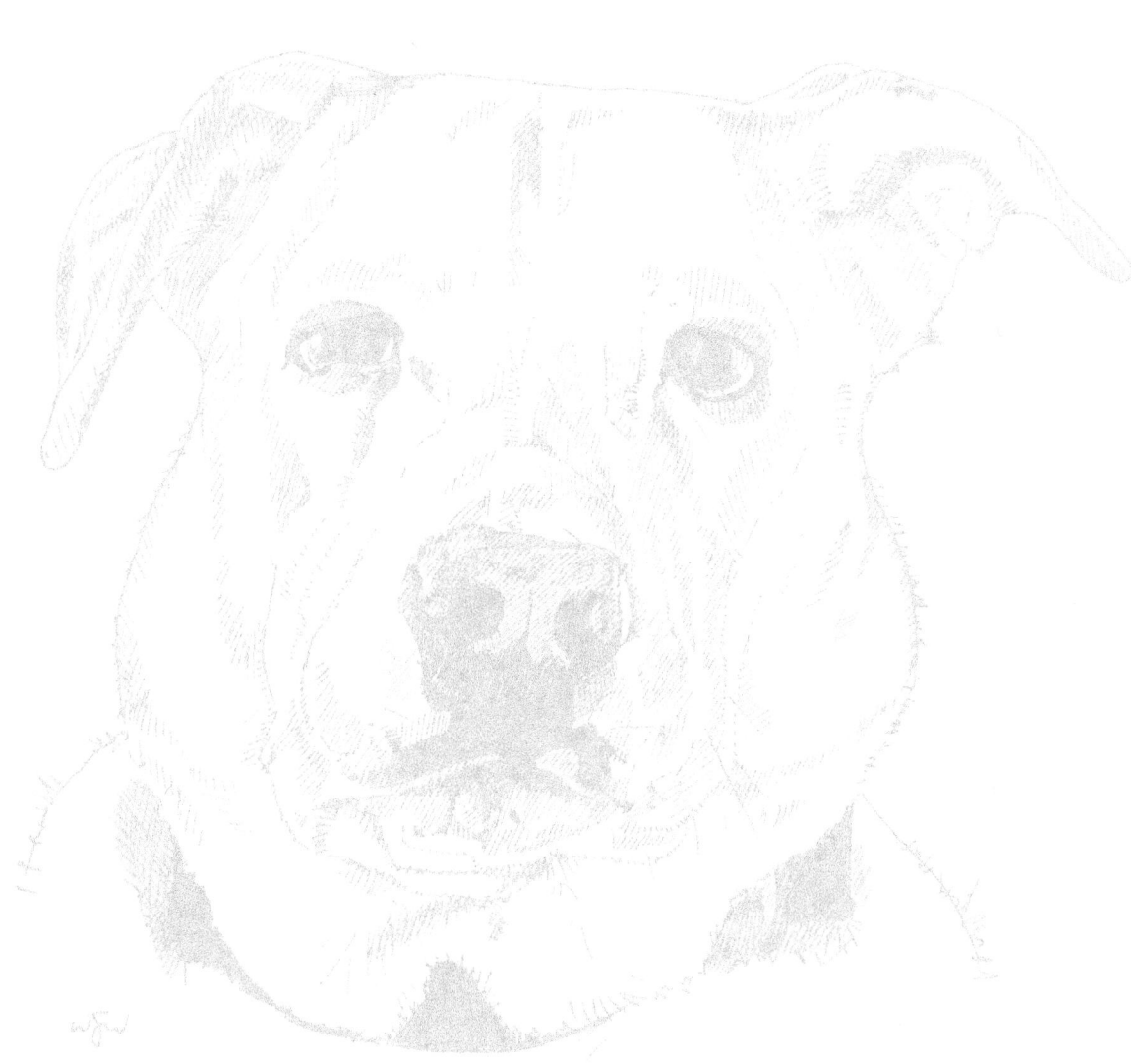

**Shauny**

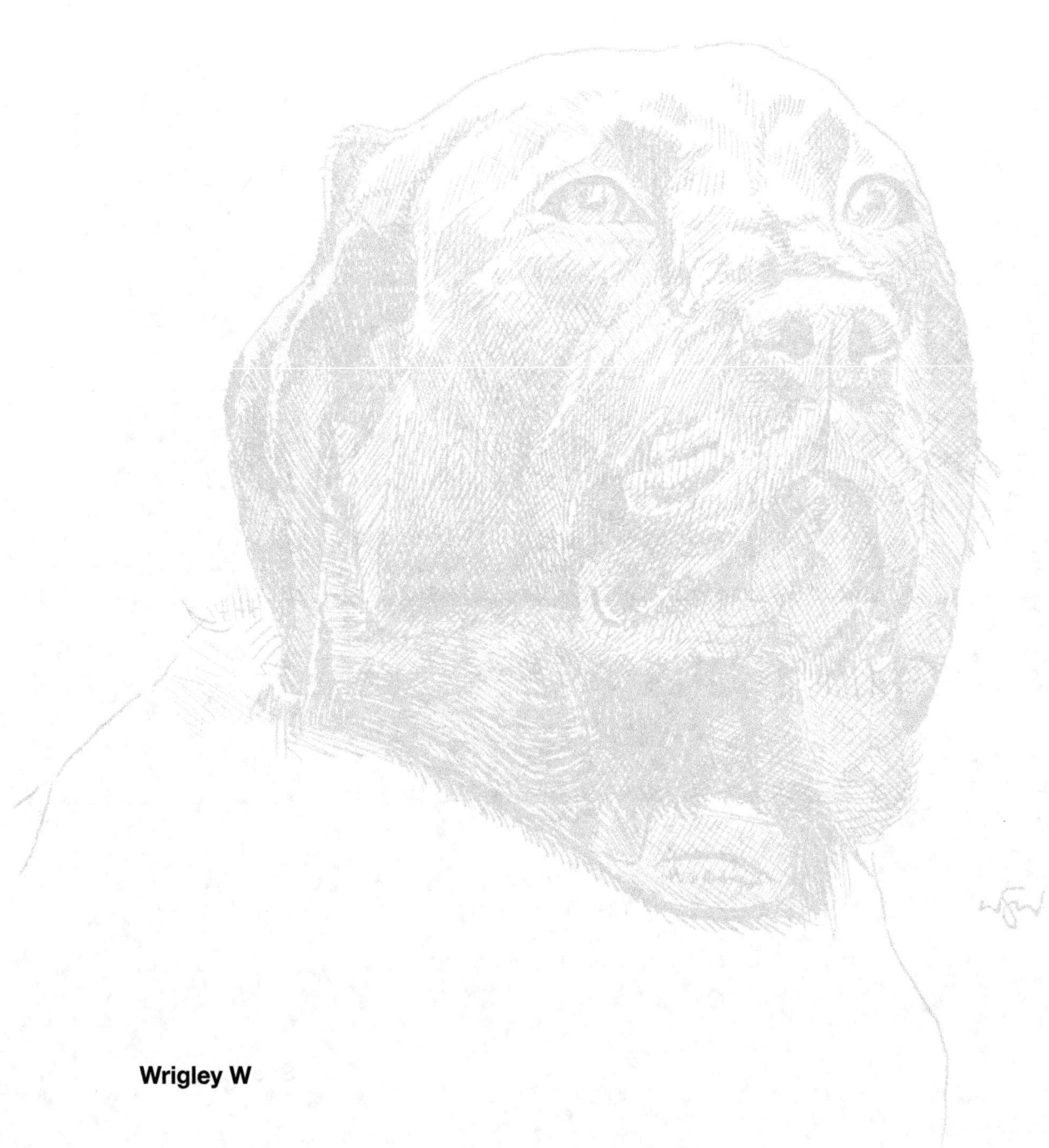

**Wrigley W**

Walter

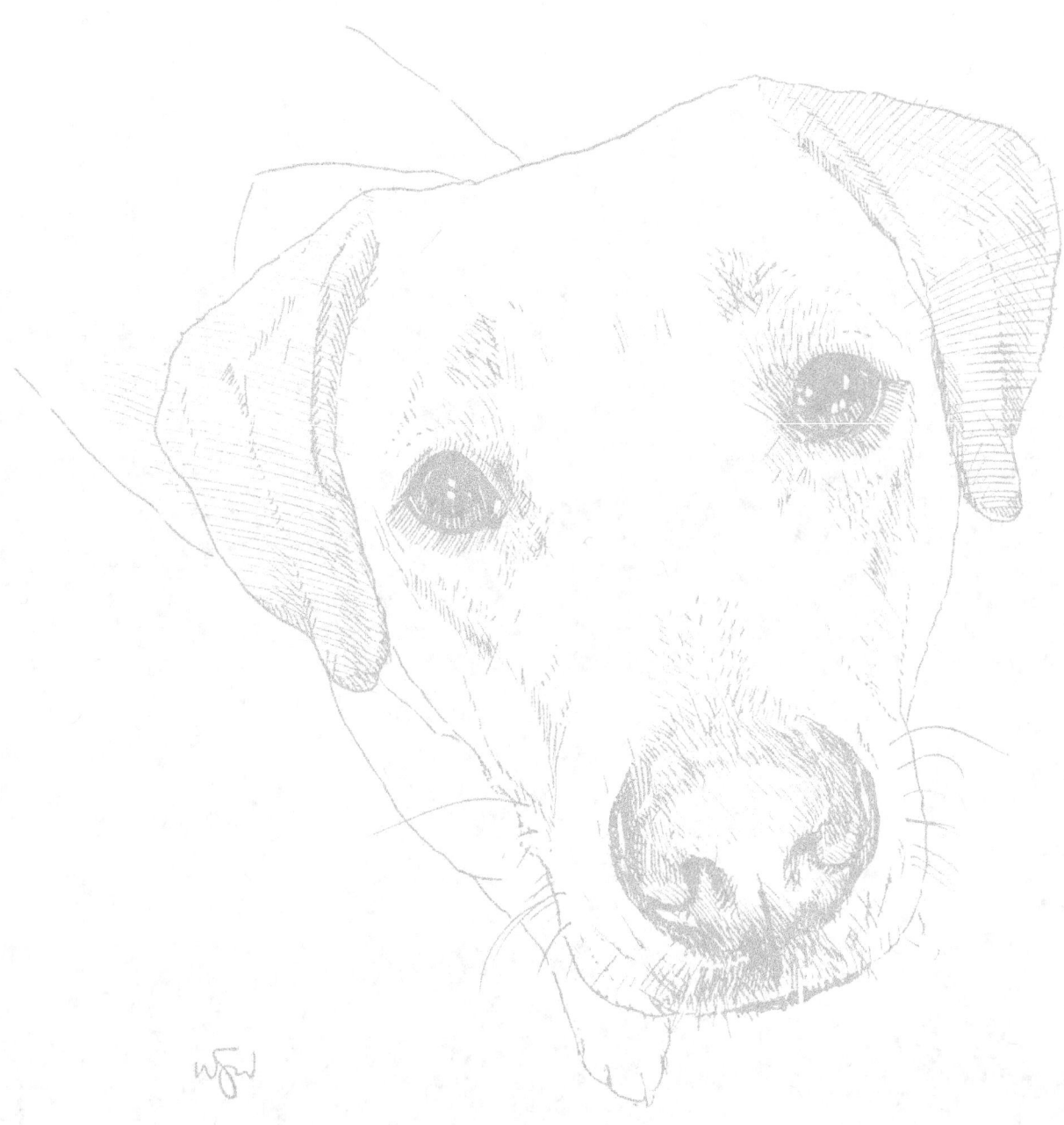

**Ellie**

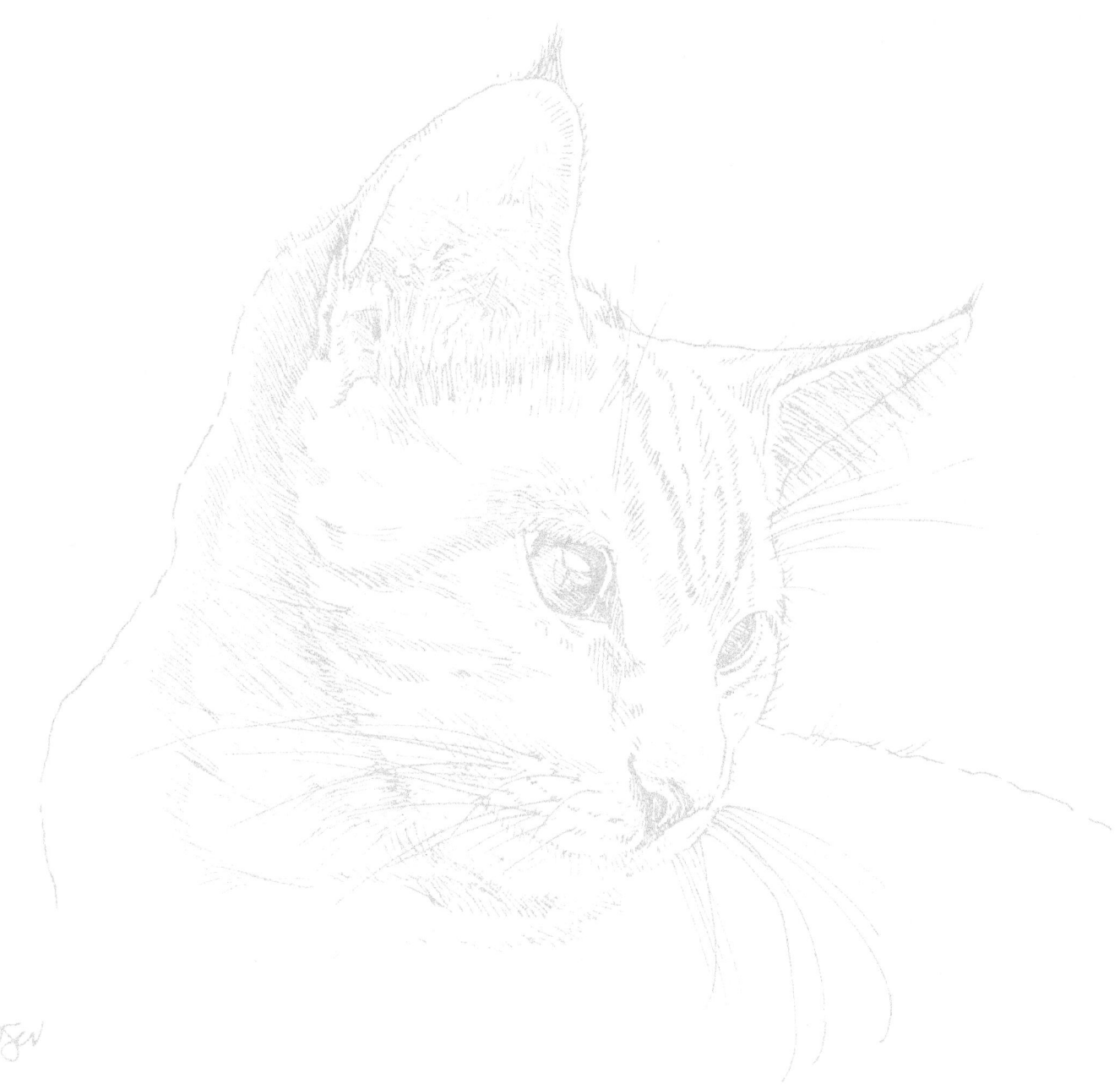

Archie

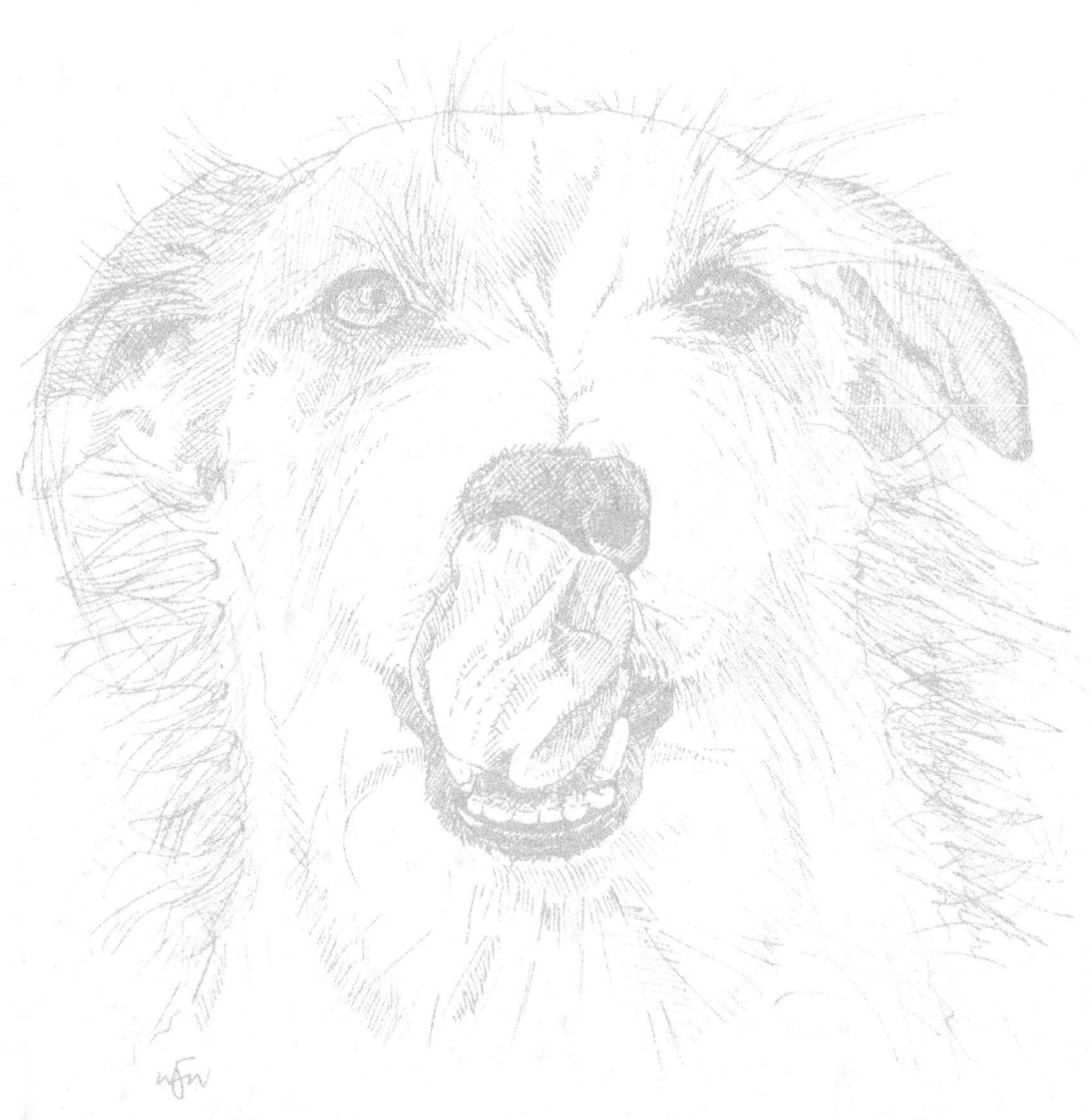

Jack

**Cardinal**

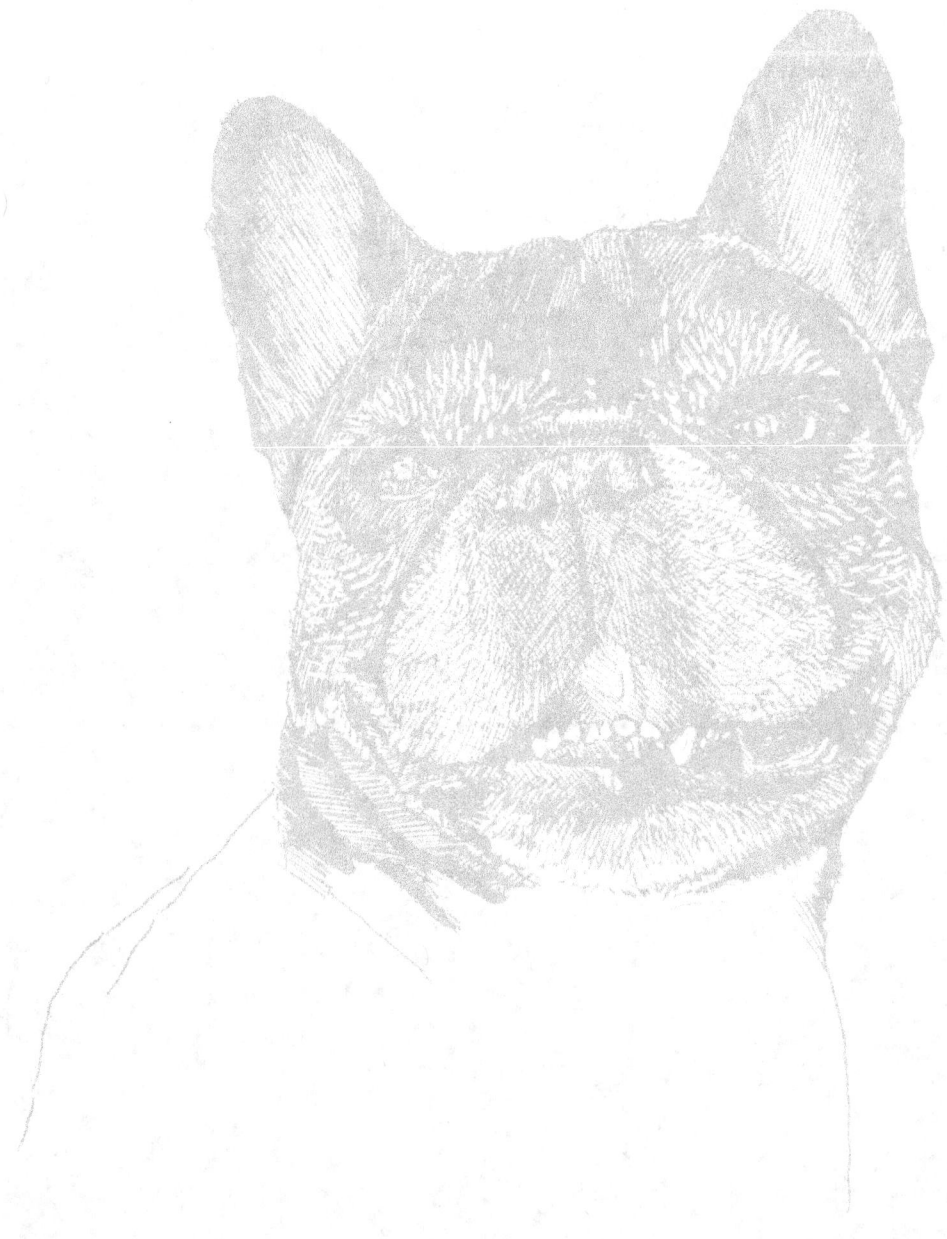

**Hank**

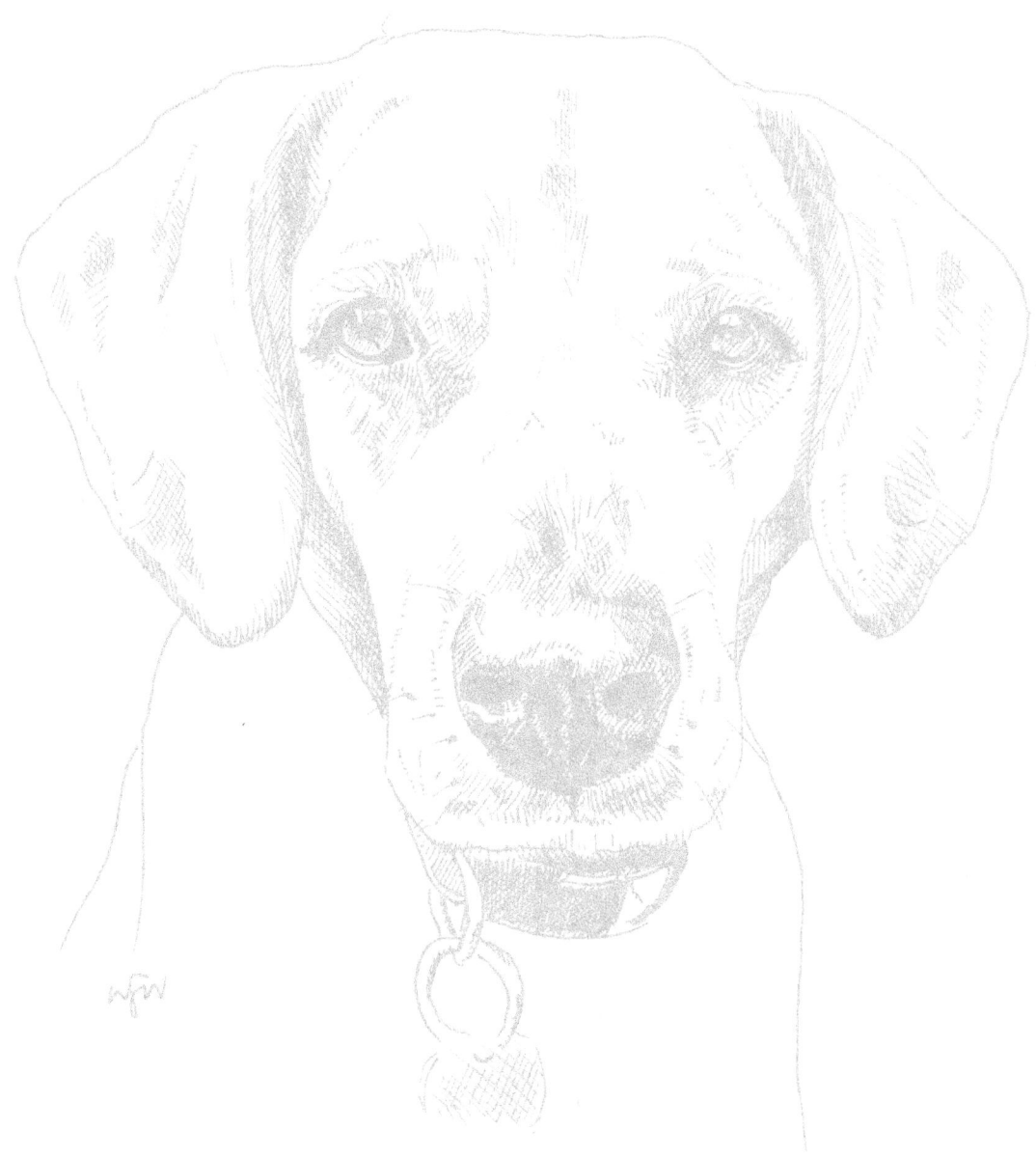

Ralphy

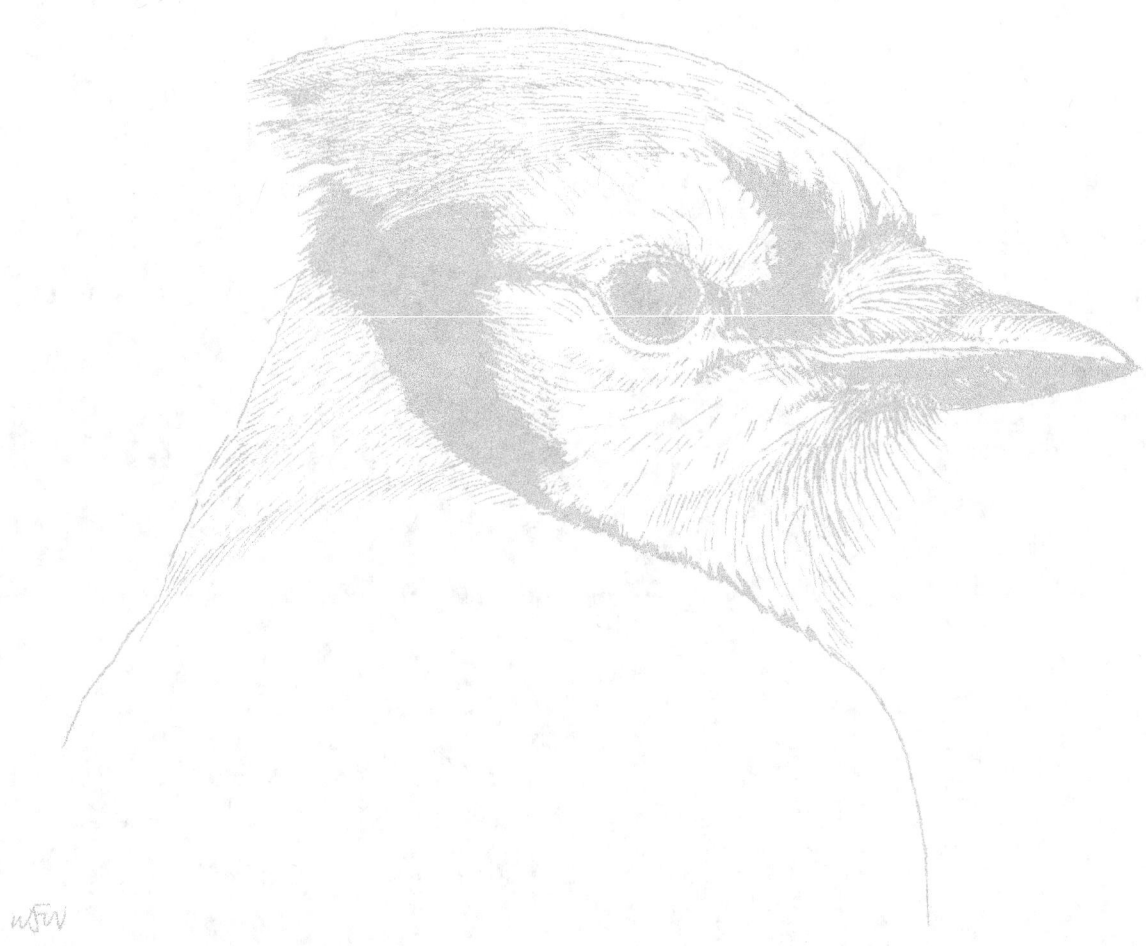

**Blue Jay**

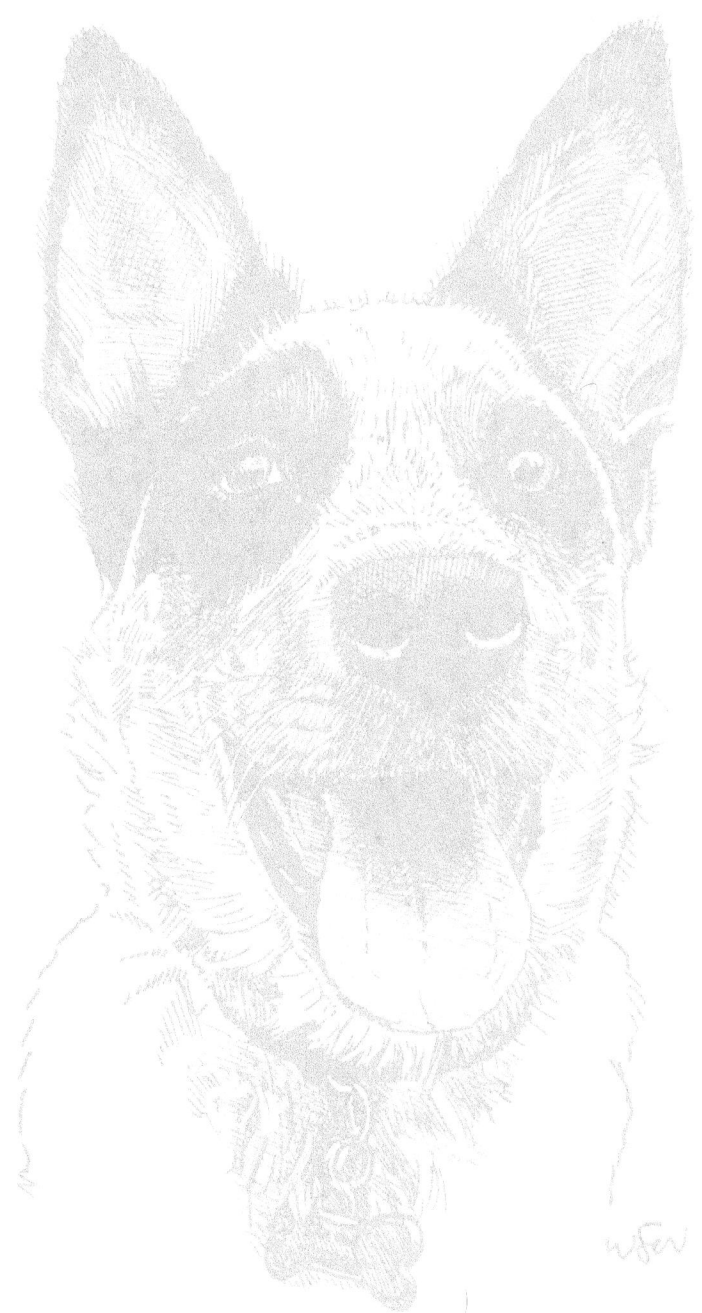

**Wahuhi**

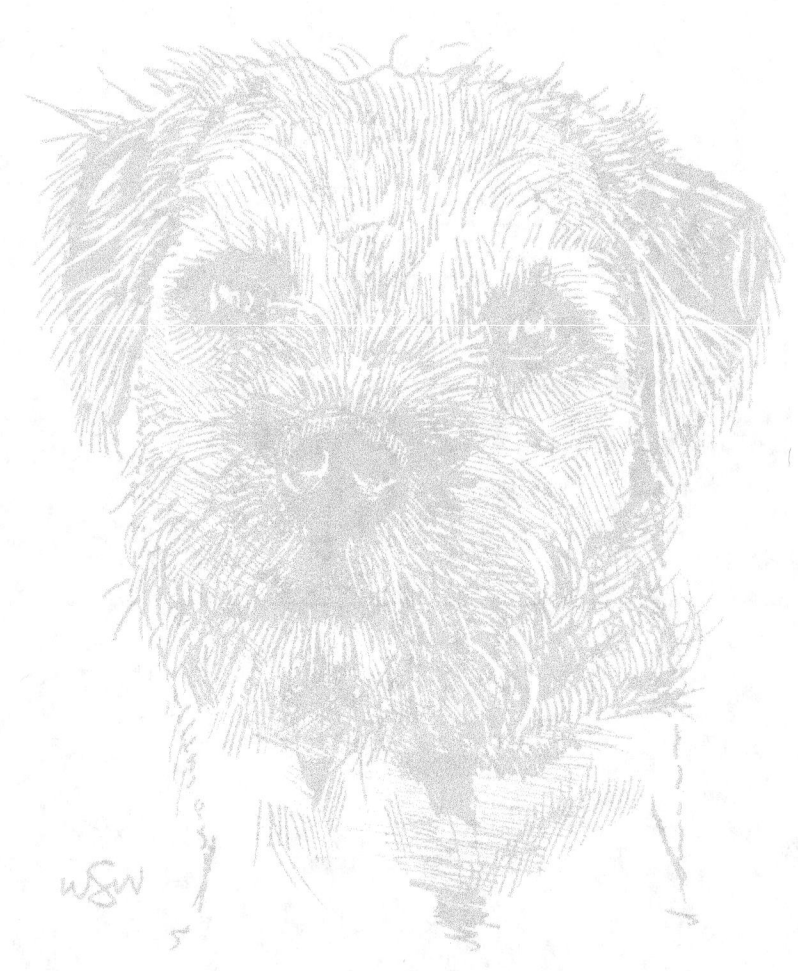

**Fred**

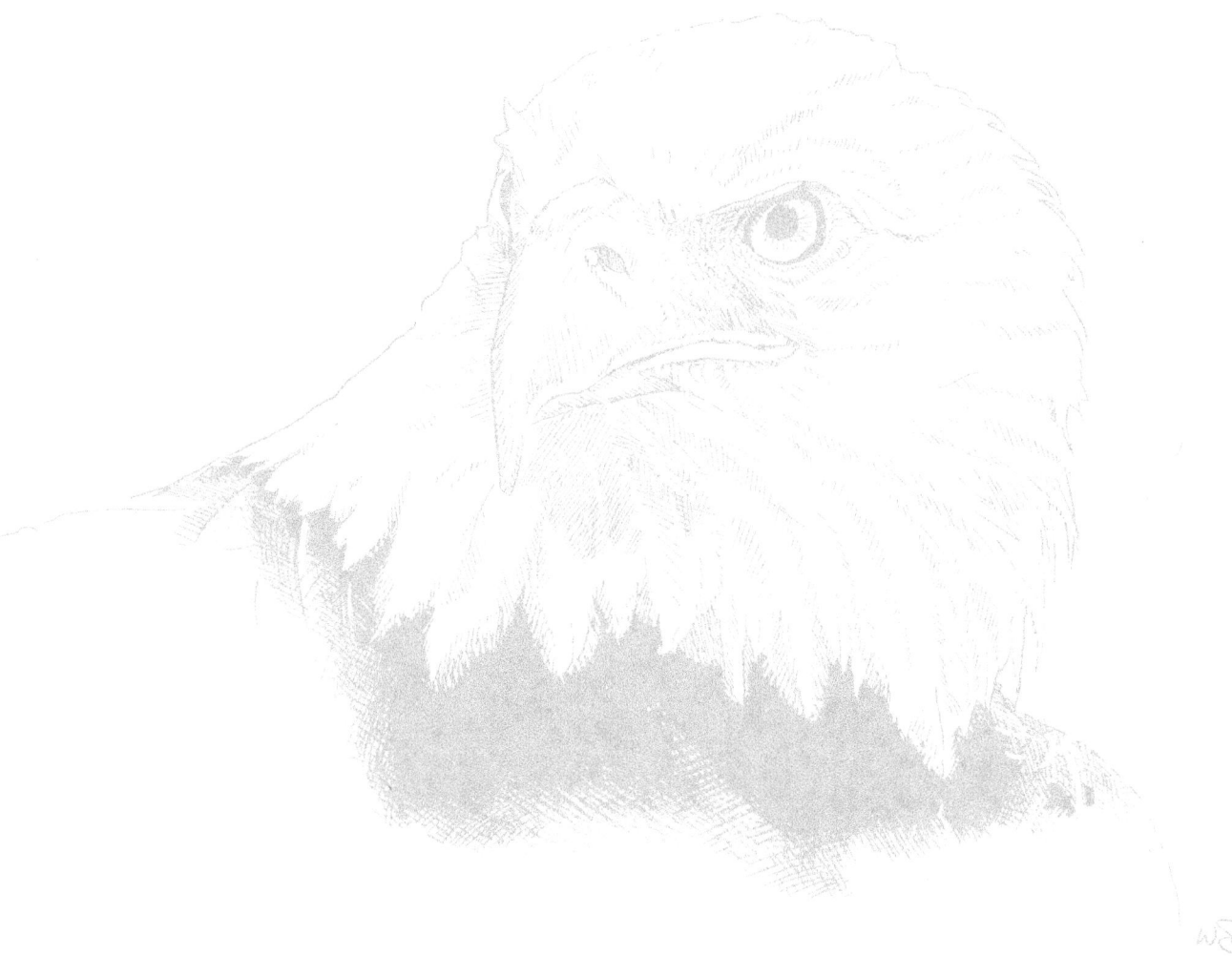

**Bald Eagle**

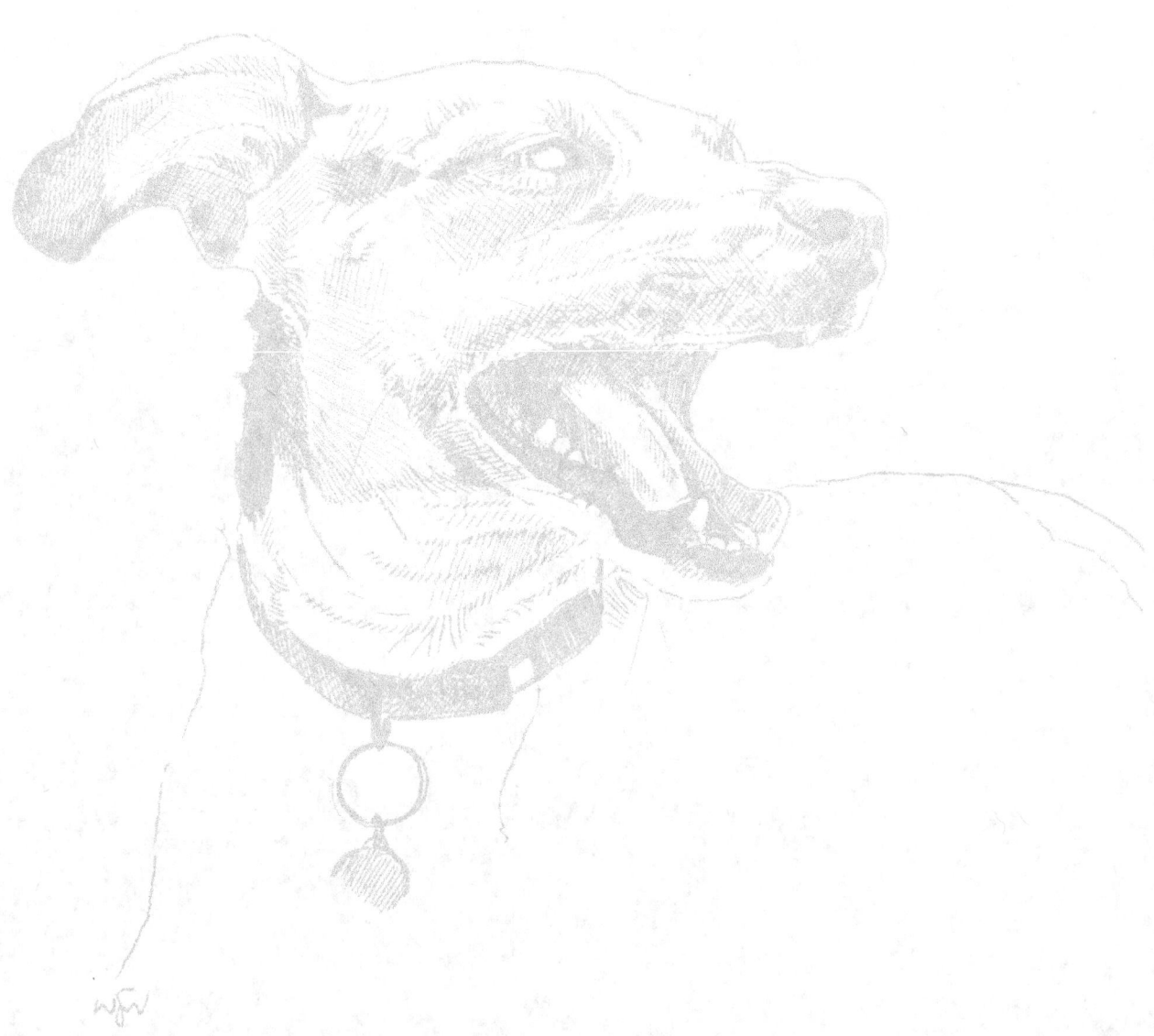

**Jolene**

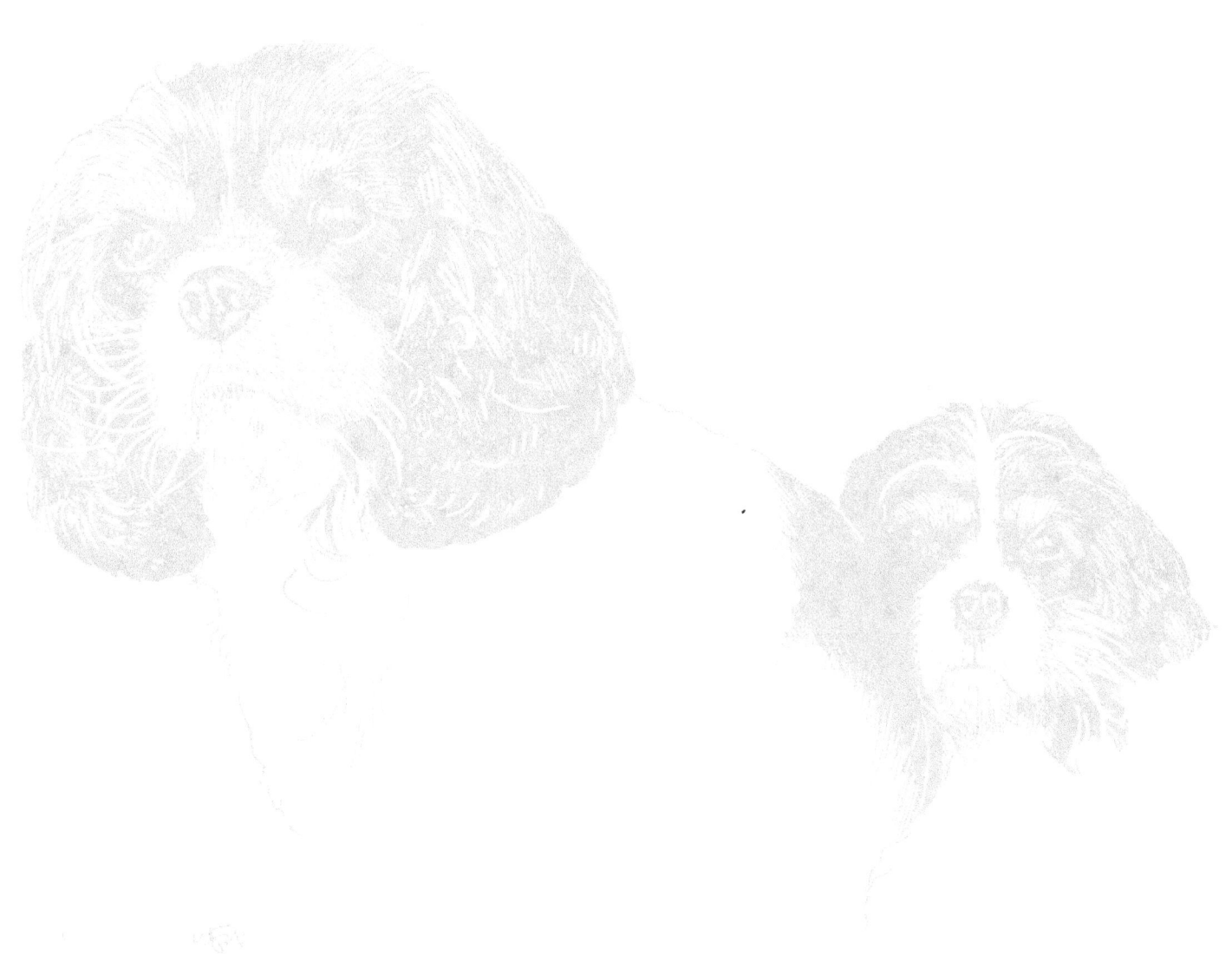

**Ruthy Mae & Betty Jean**

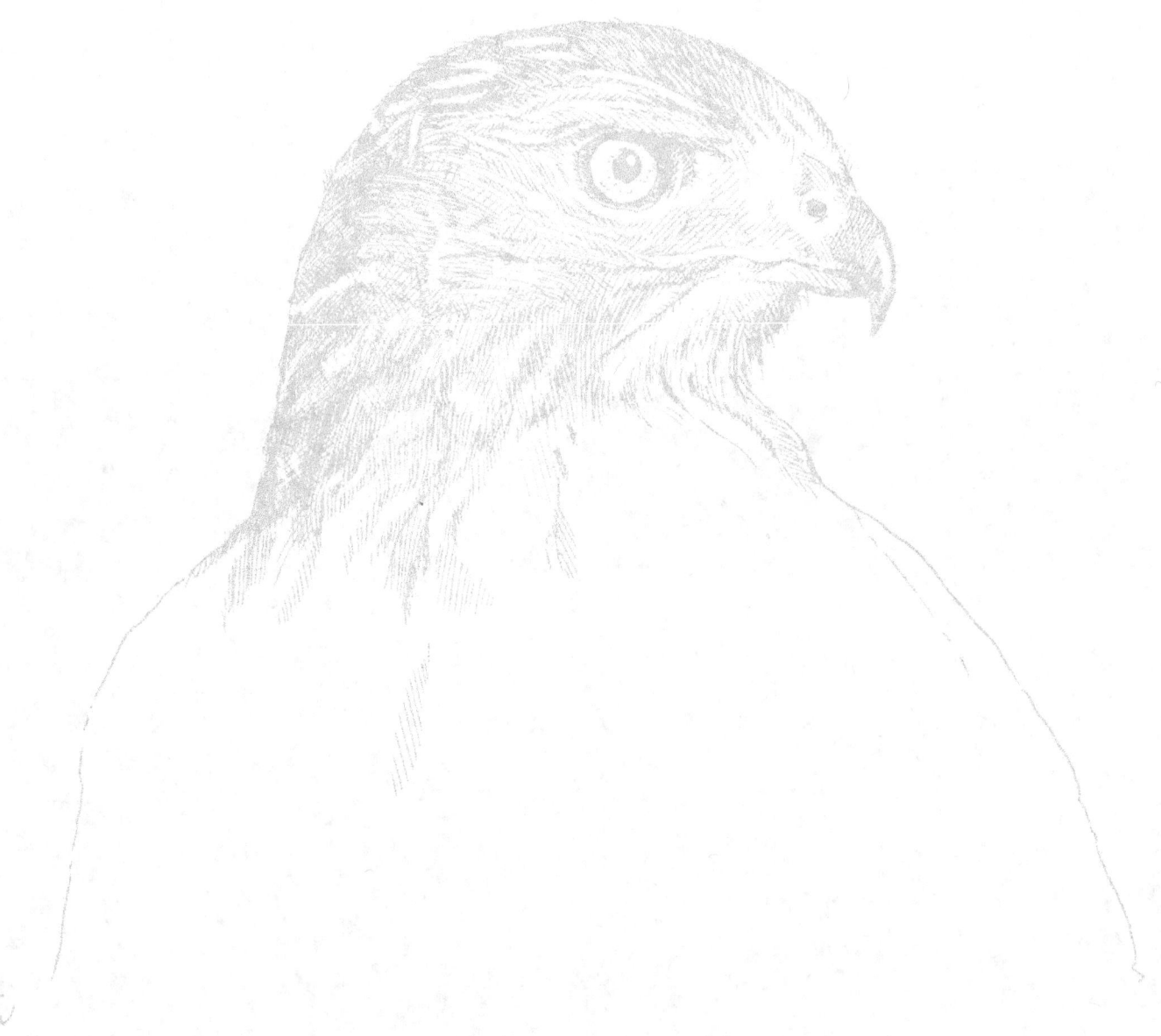

**Red-Tail Hawk**

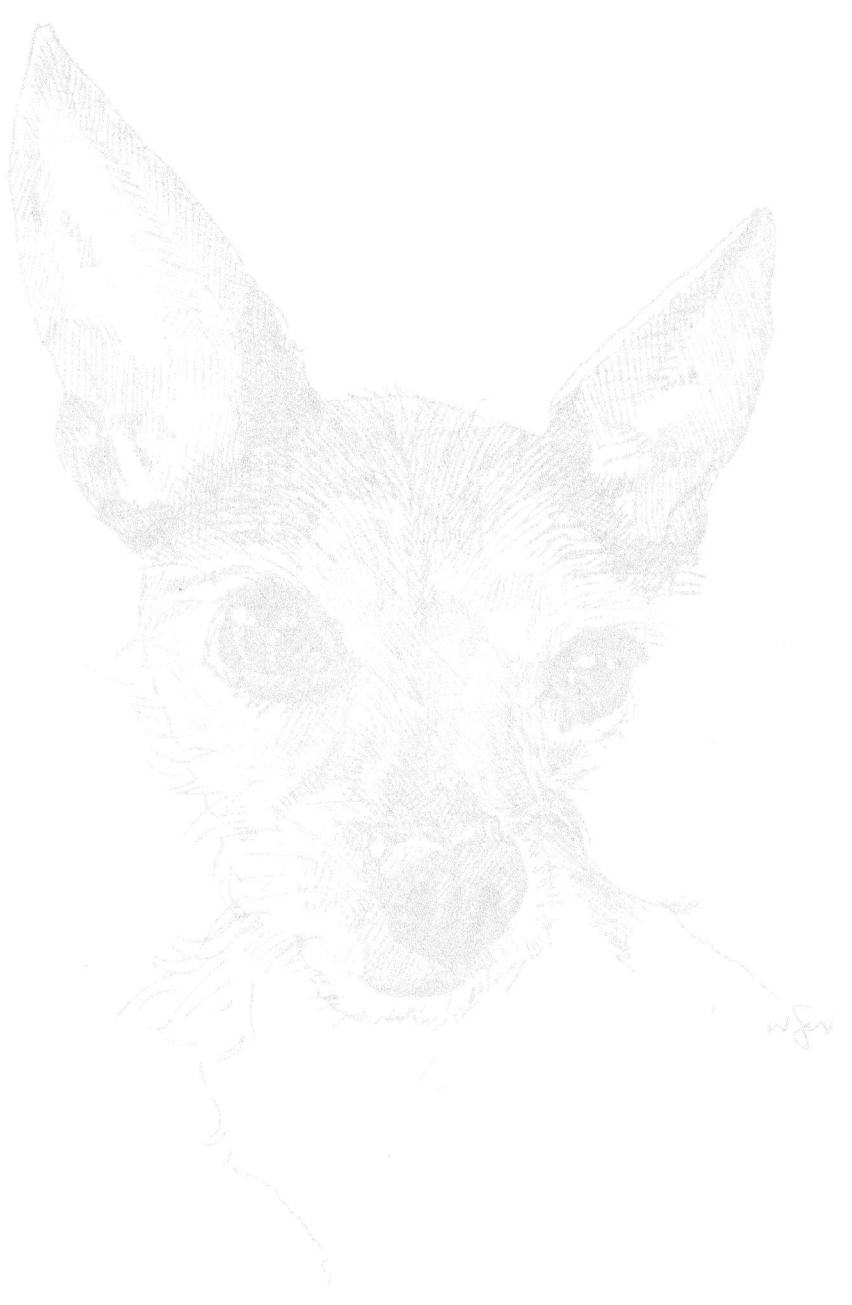

Sloane

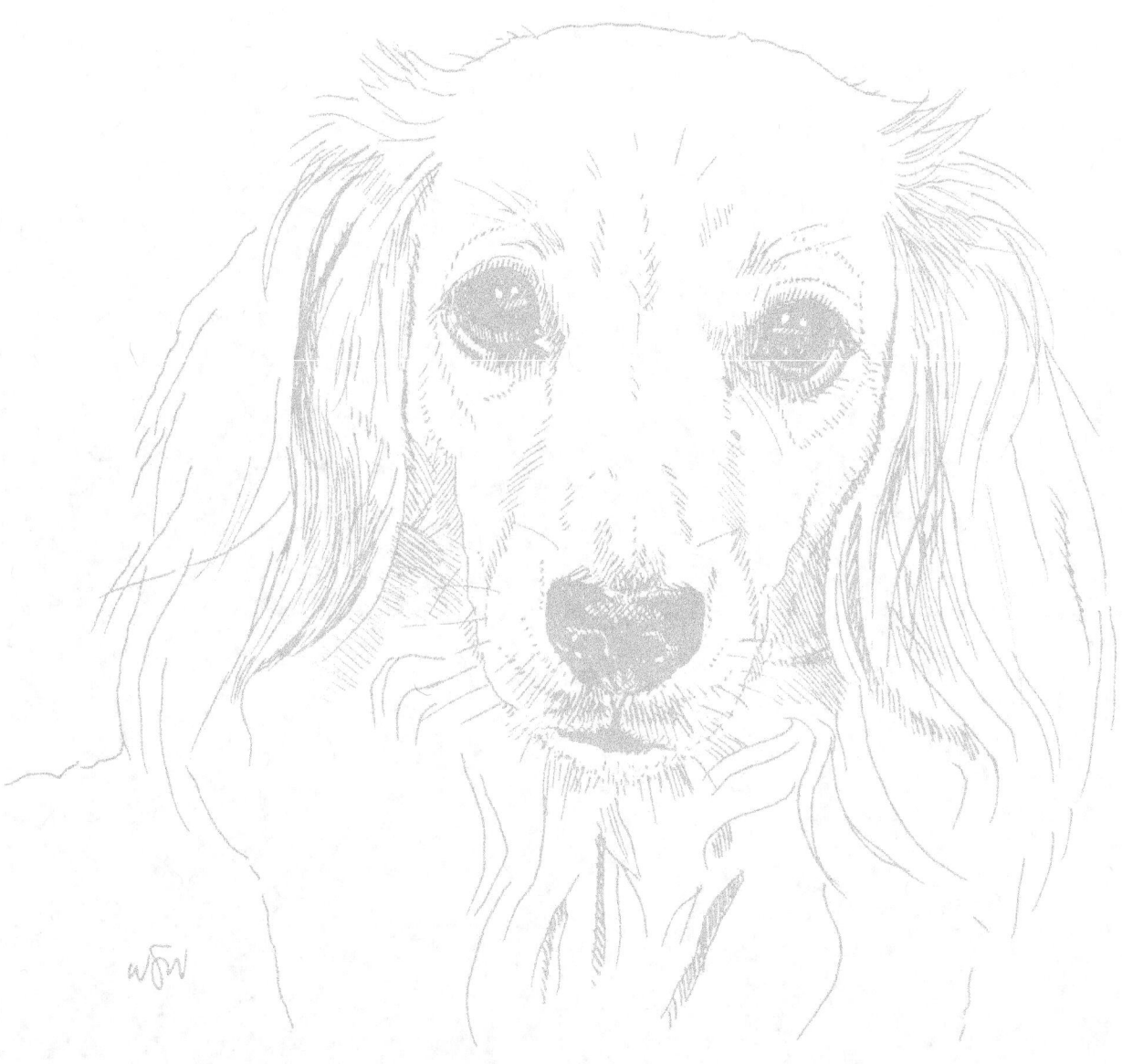

**Hazel**

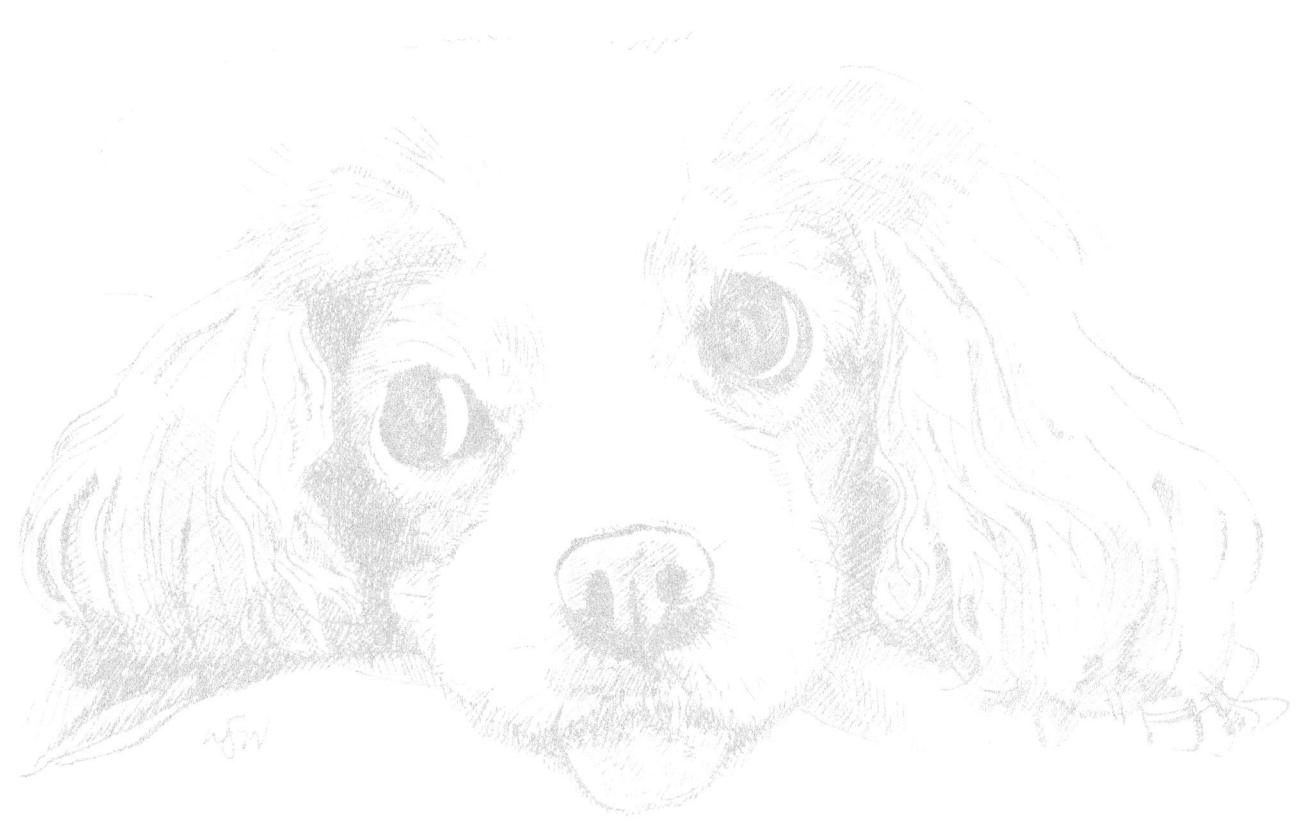

Suzette

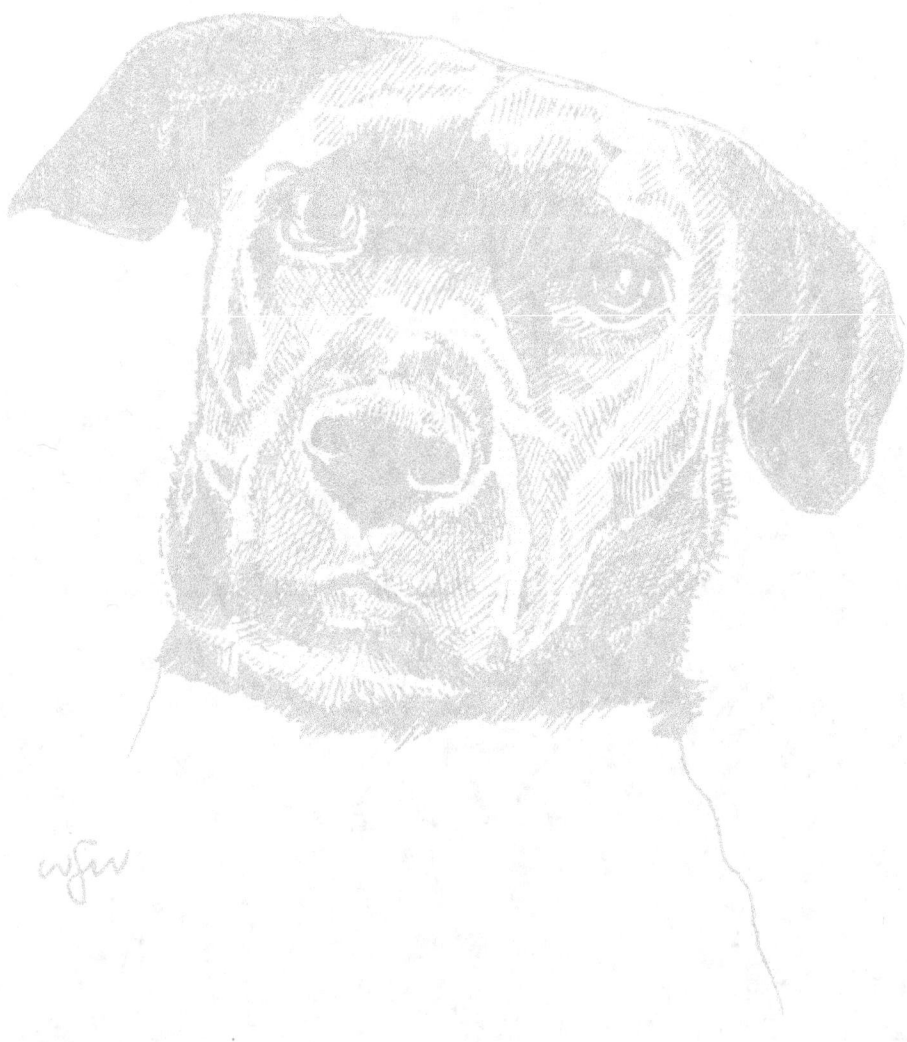

**Phoebe**

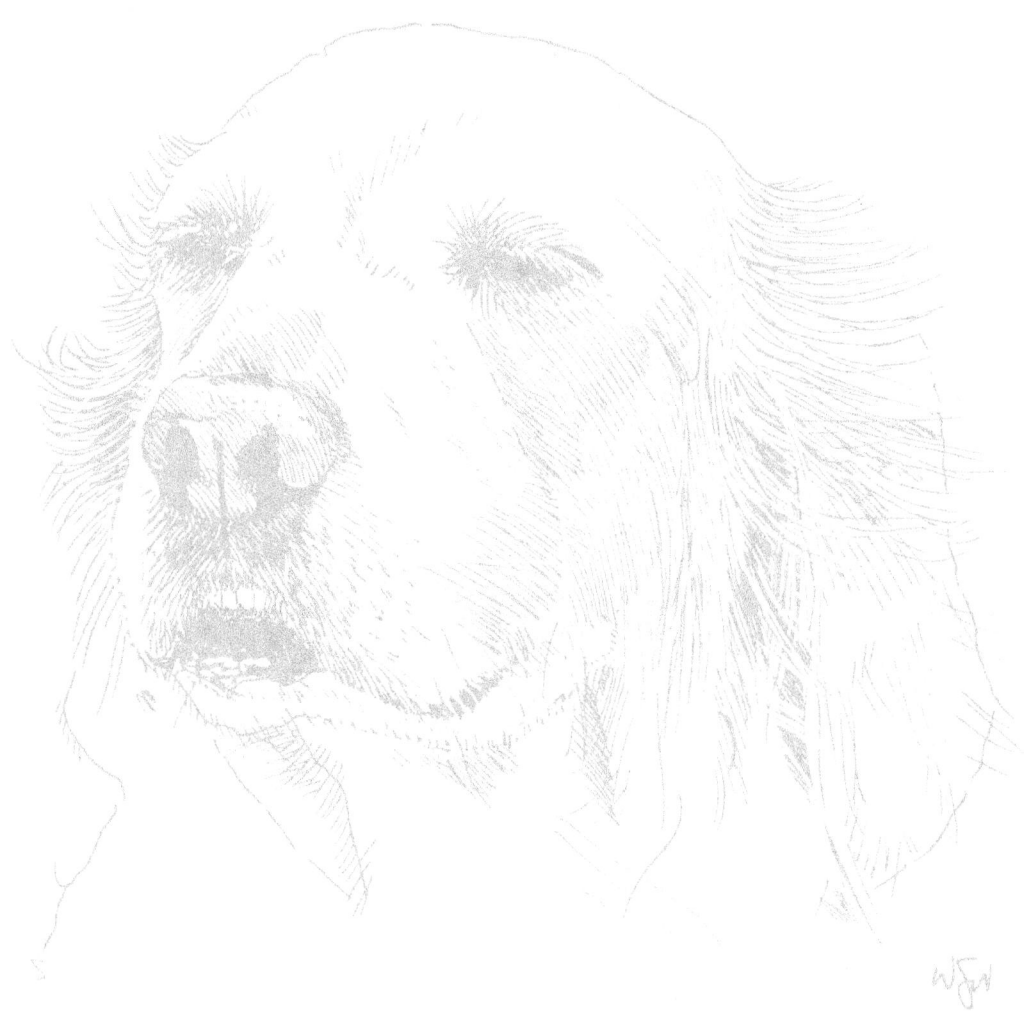

**Lola**

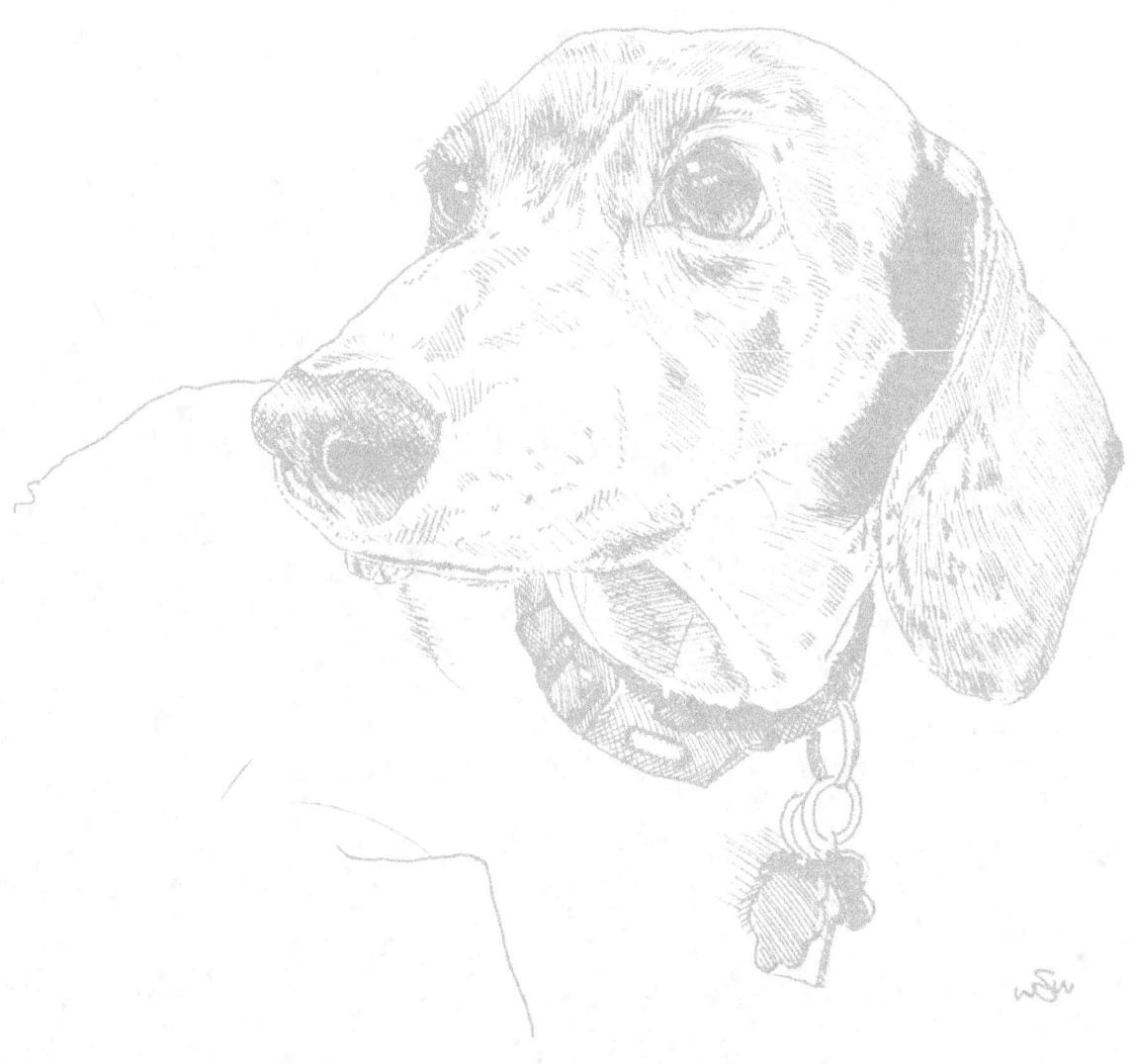

**Nimble**

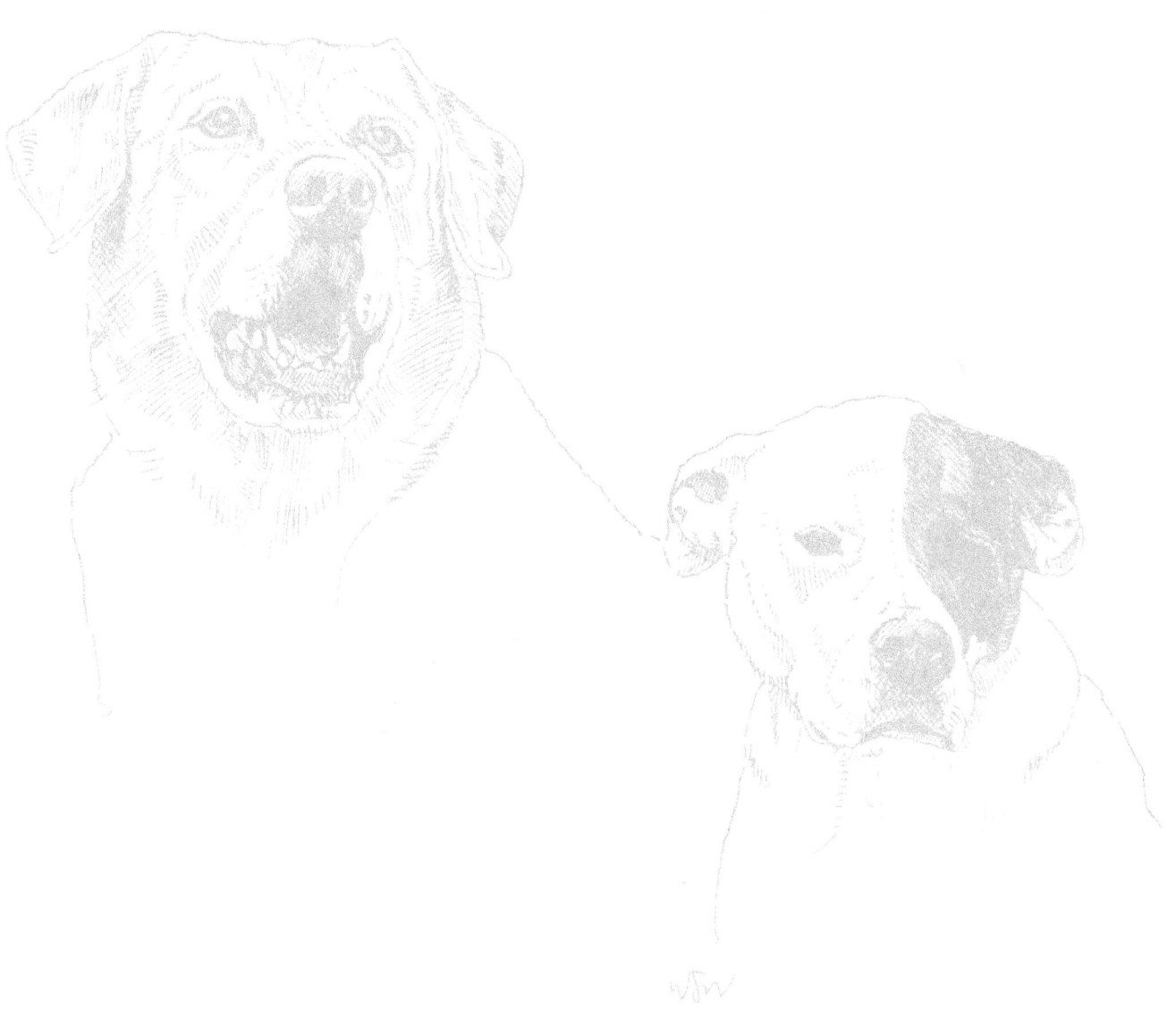

**George & Gidget**

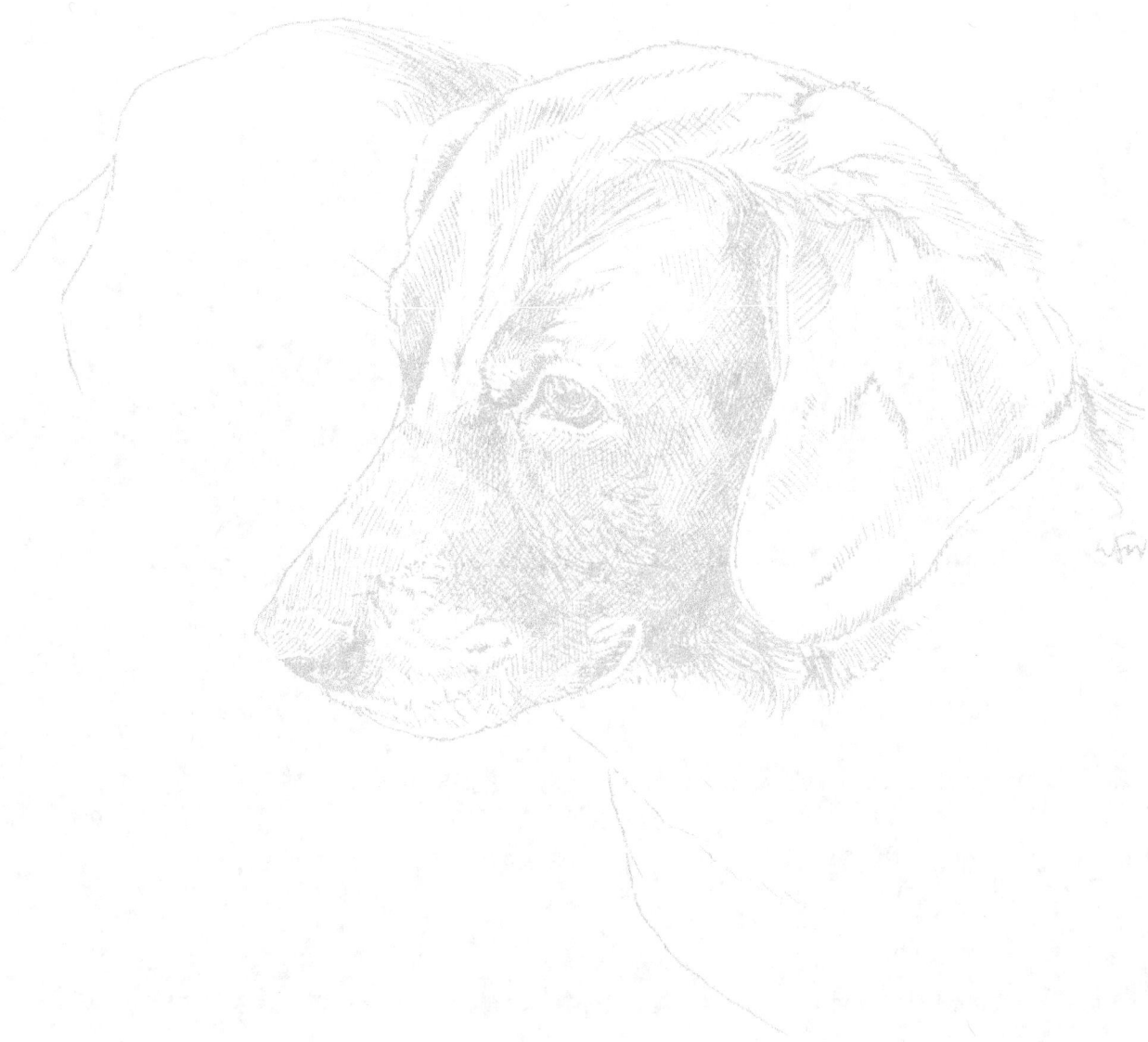

Charlie

**Pepper**

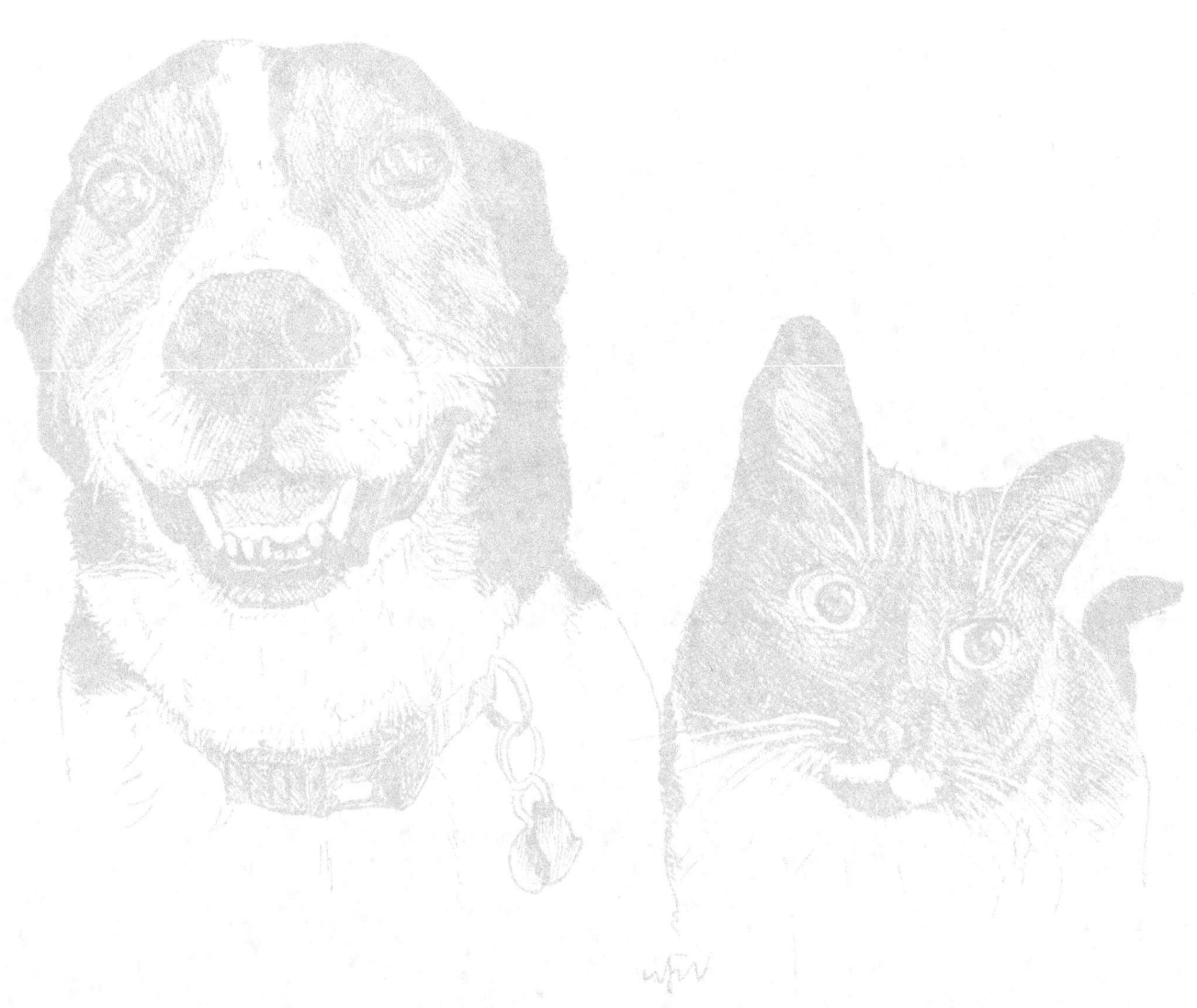

**Petey & Rupert**

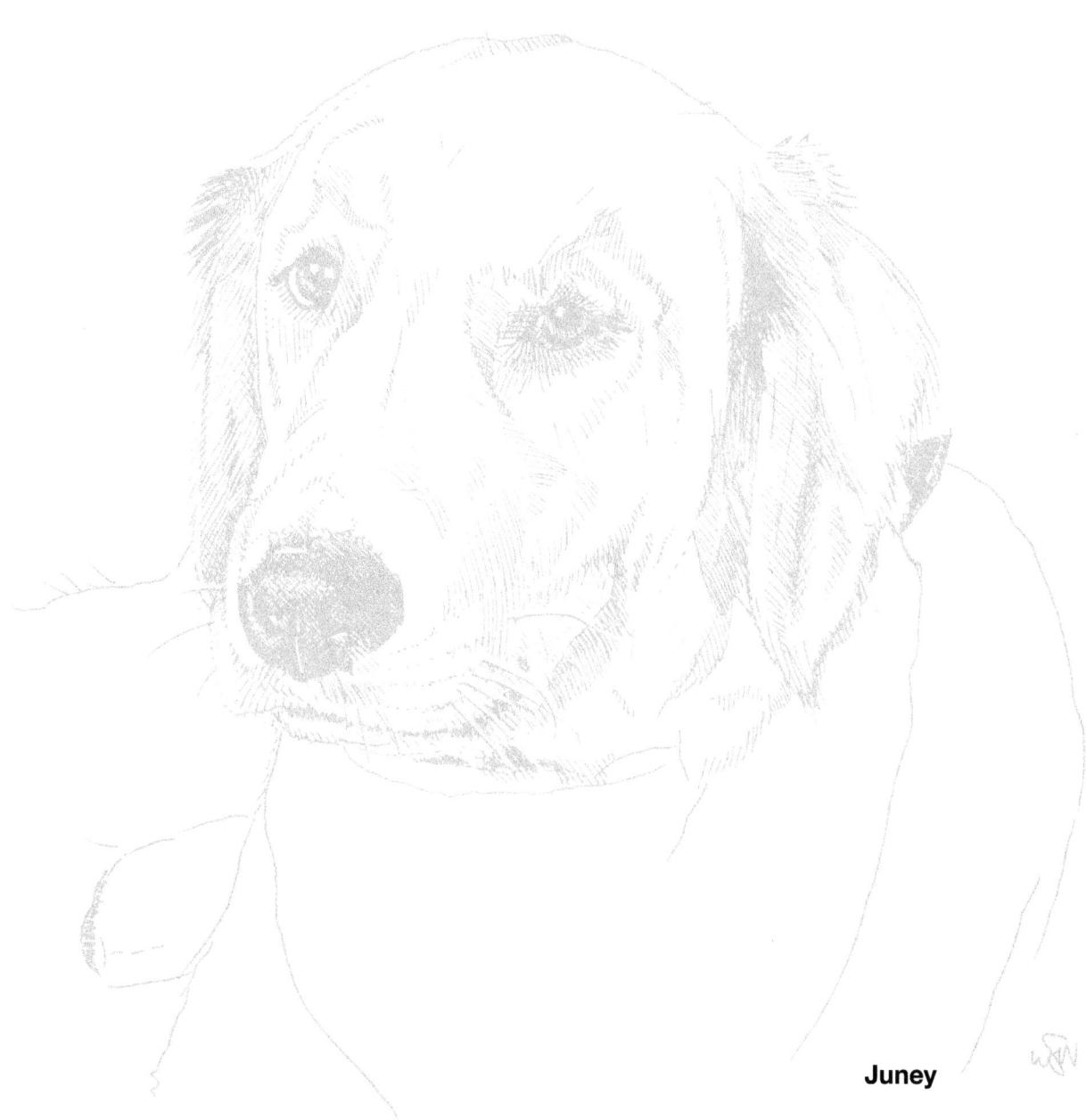

Juney

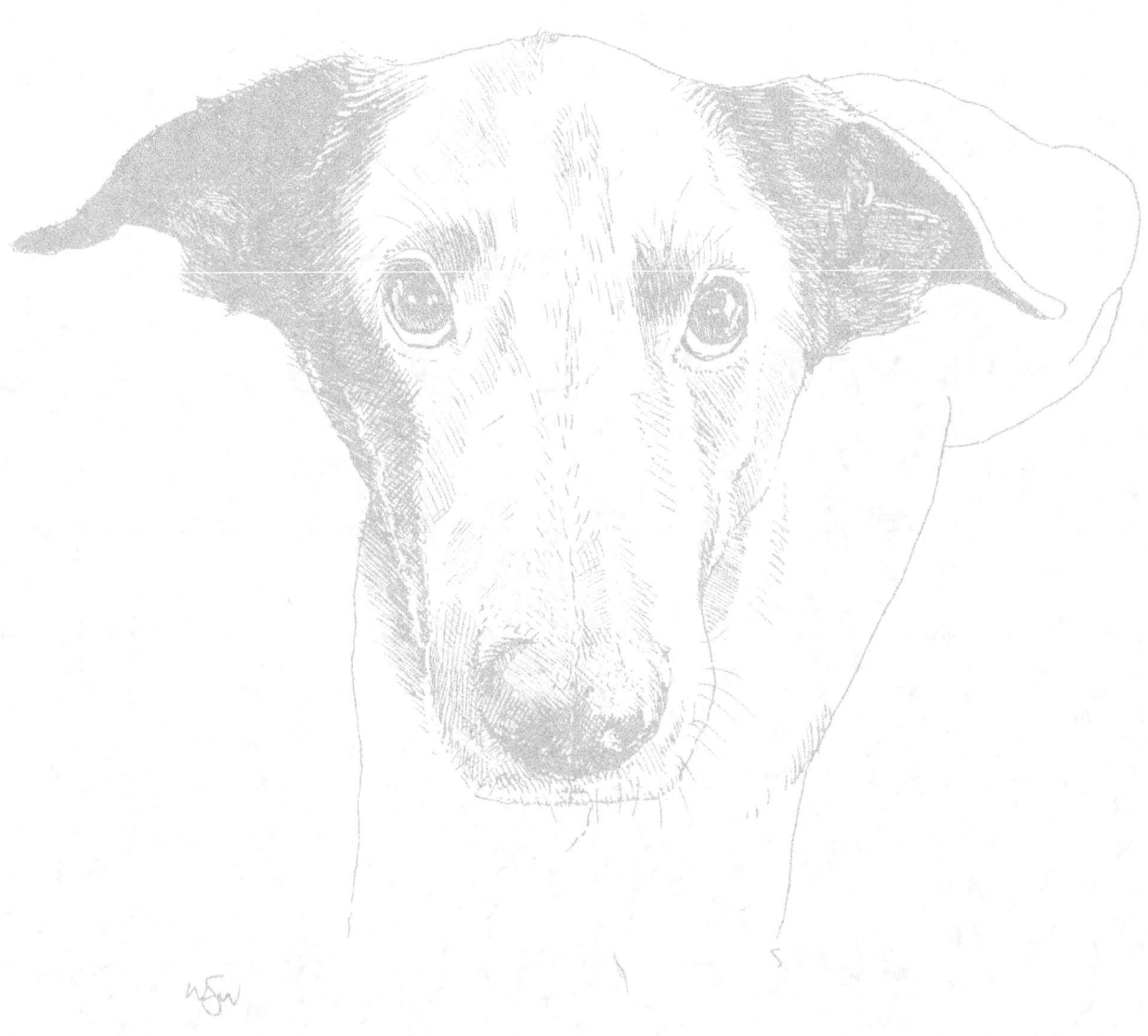

**Murray**

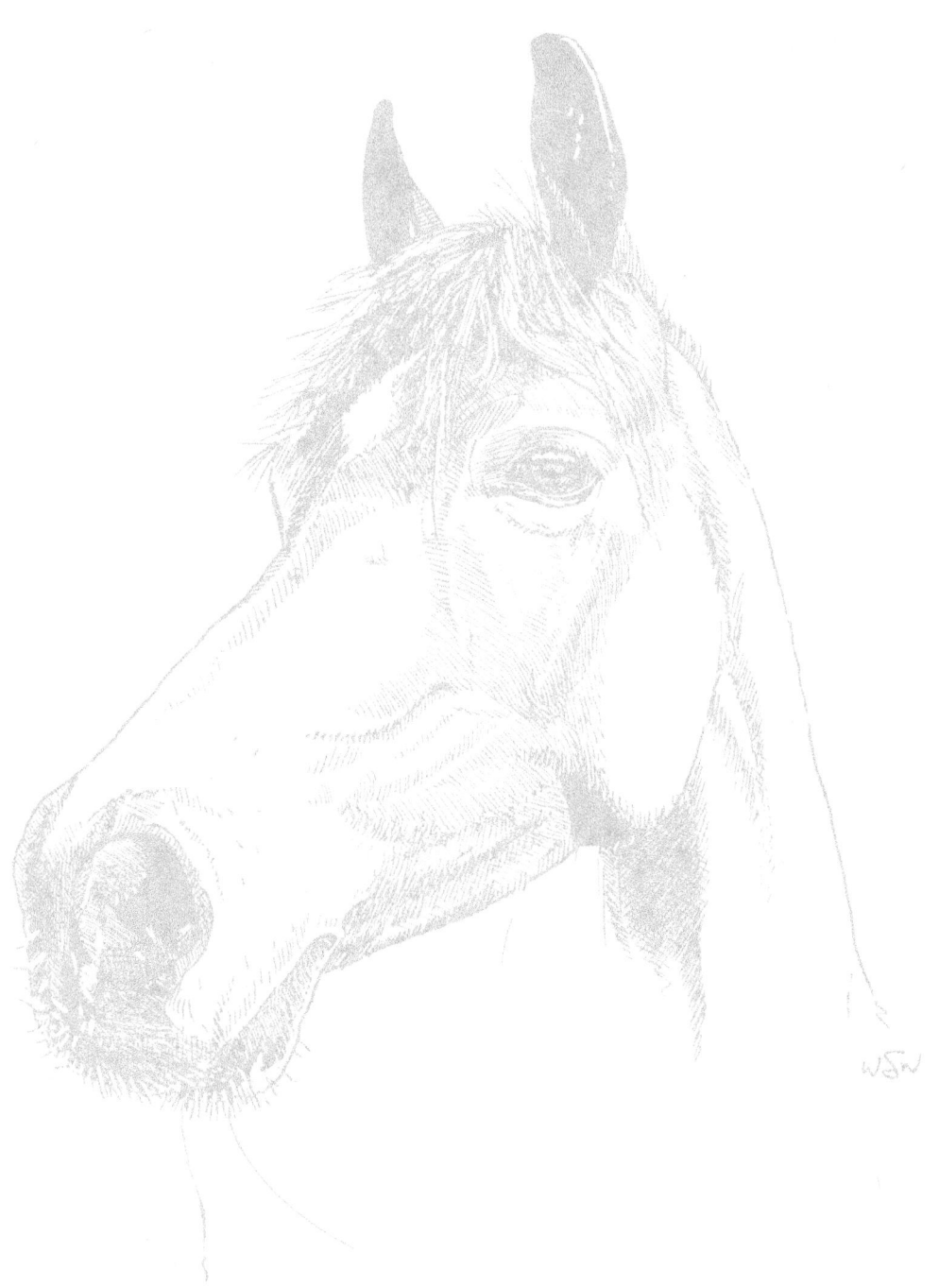

**Benjamin**

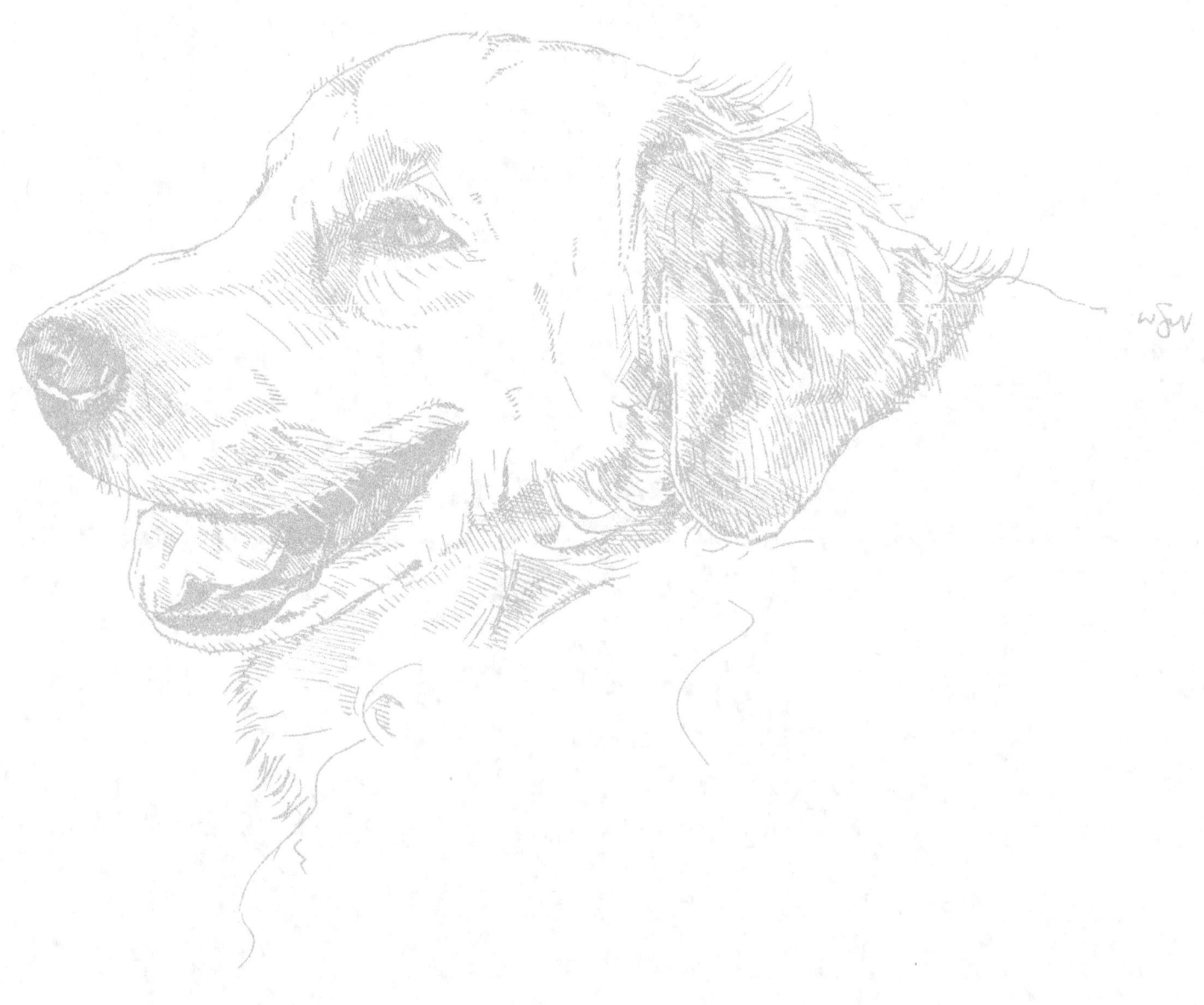

**Neil**

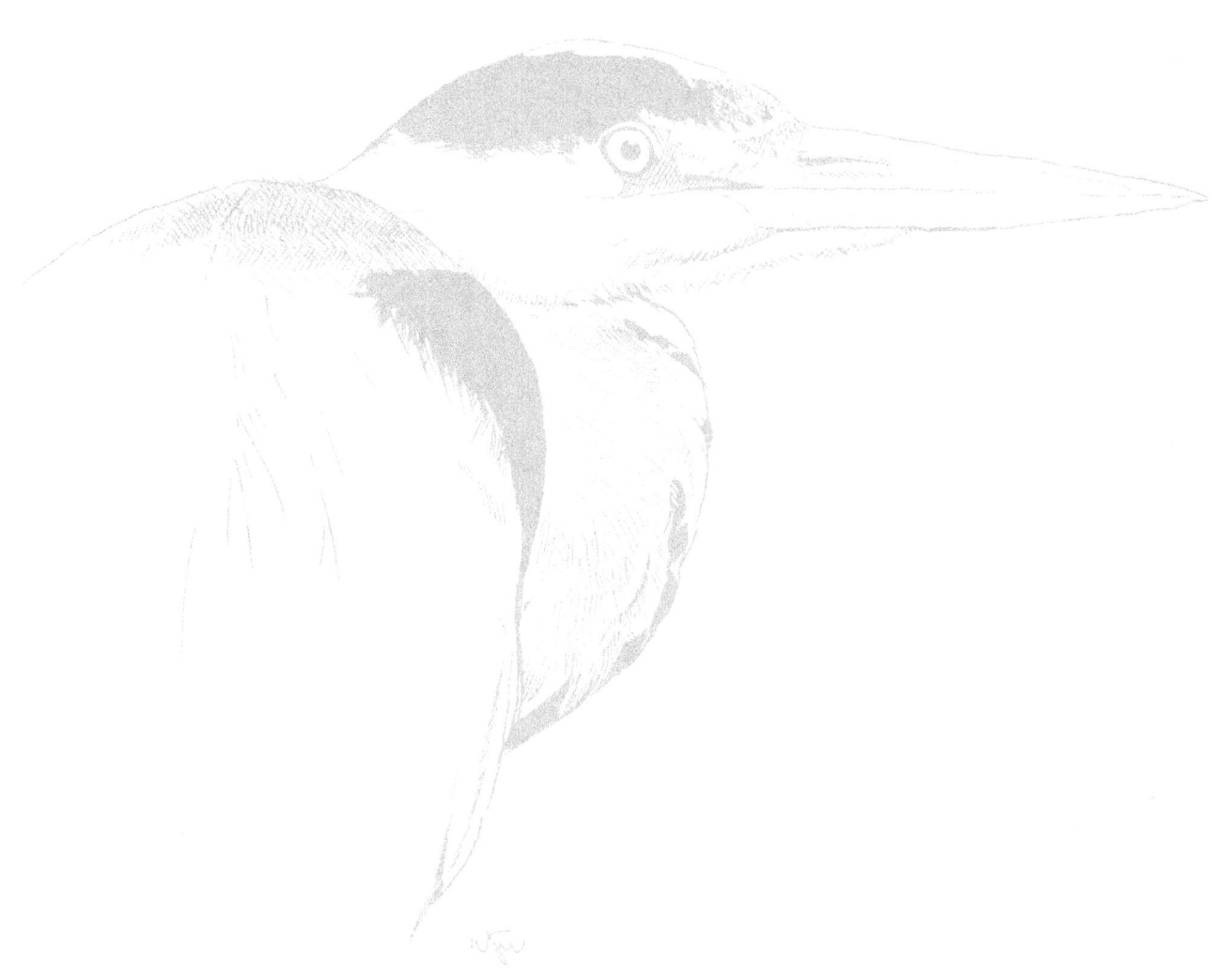

**Blue Heron**

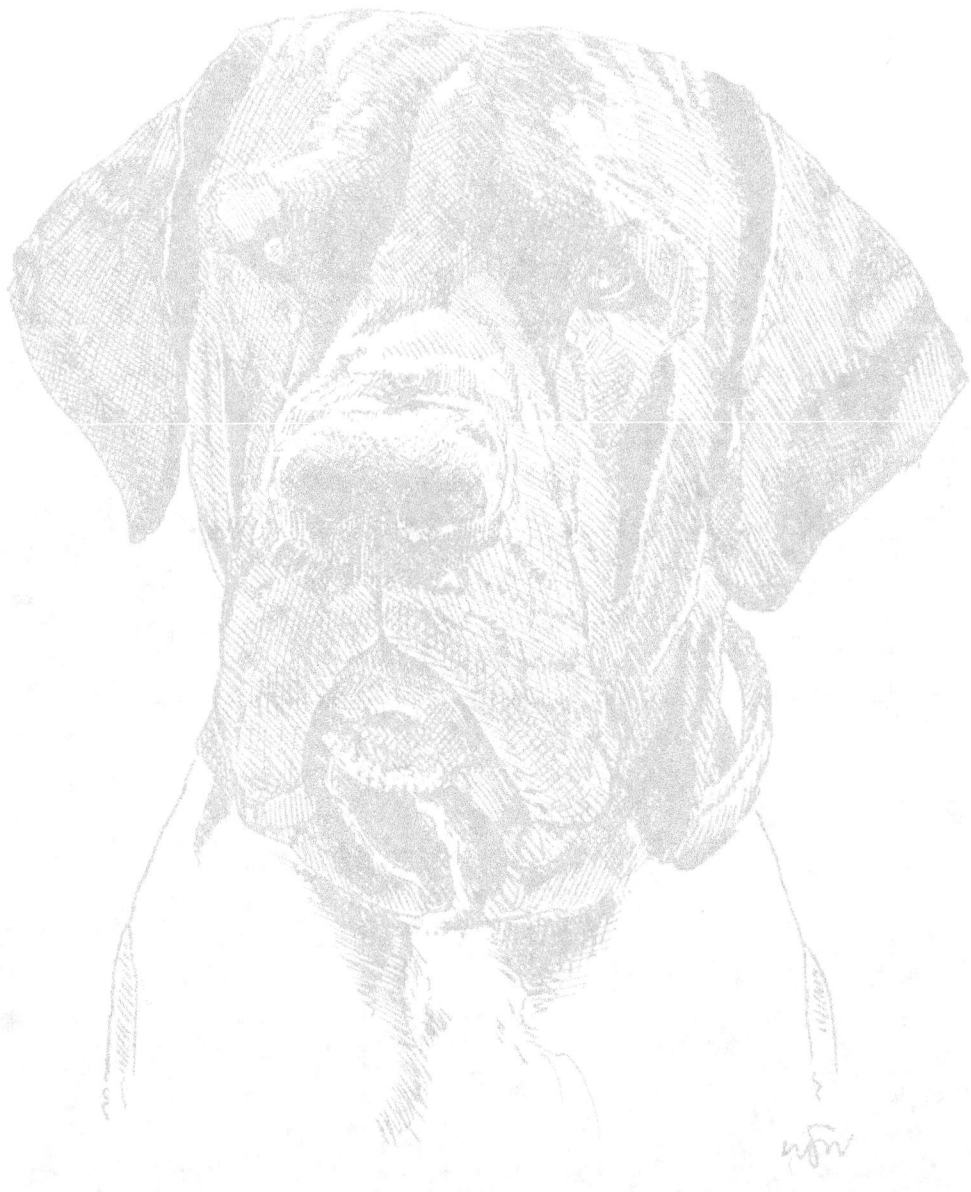

**Venom**

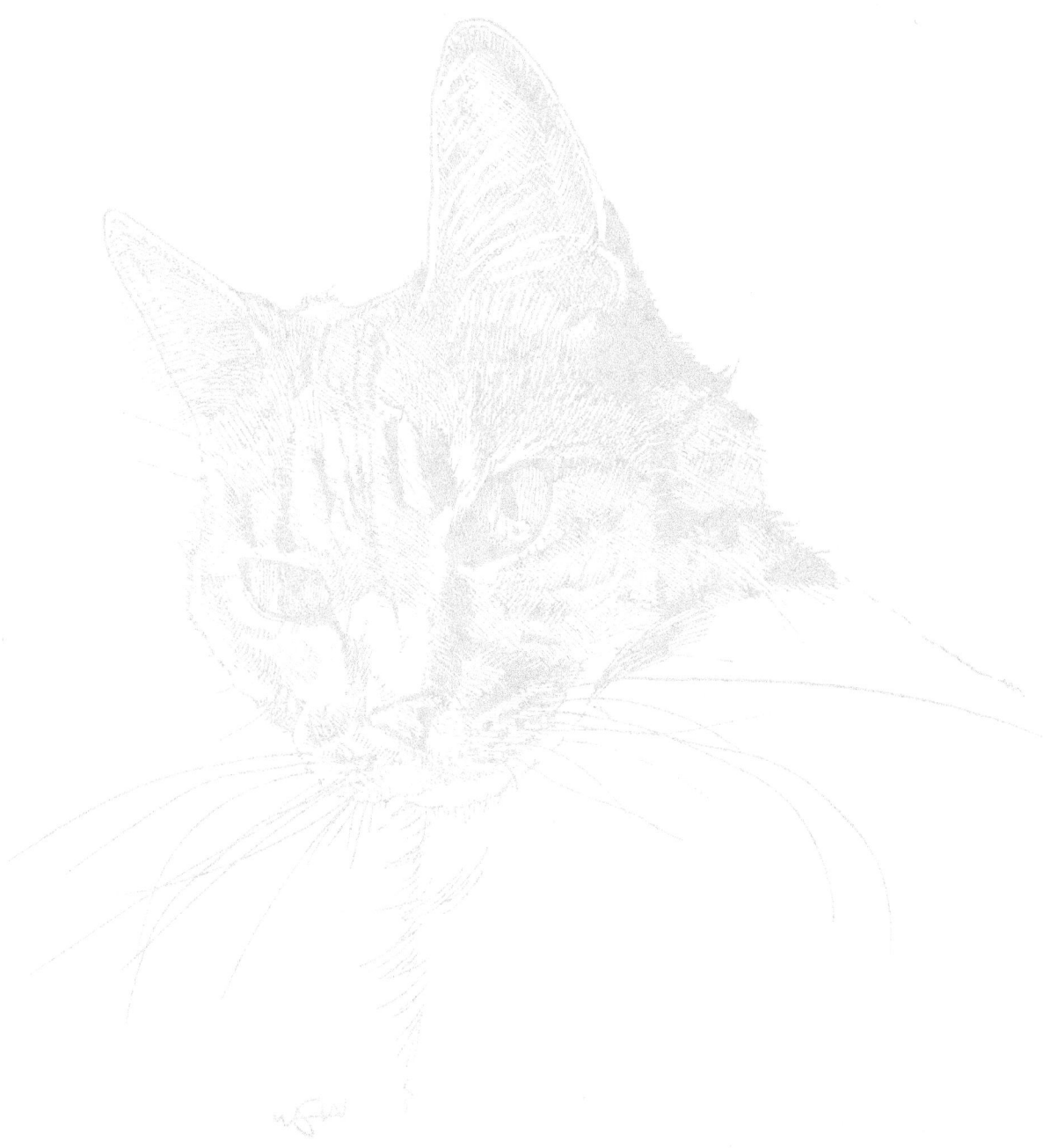

C. Cat

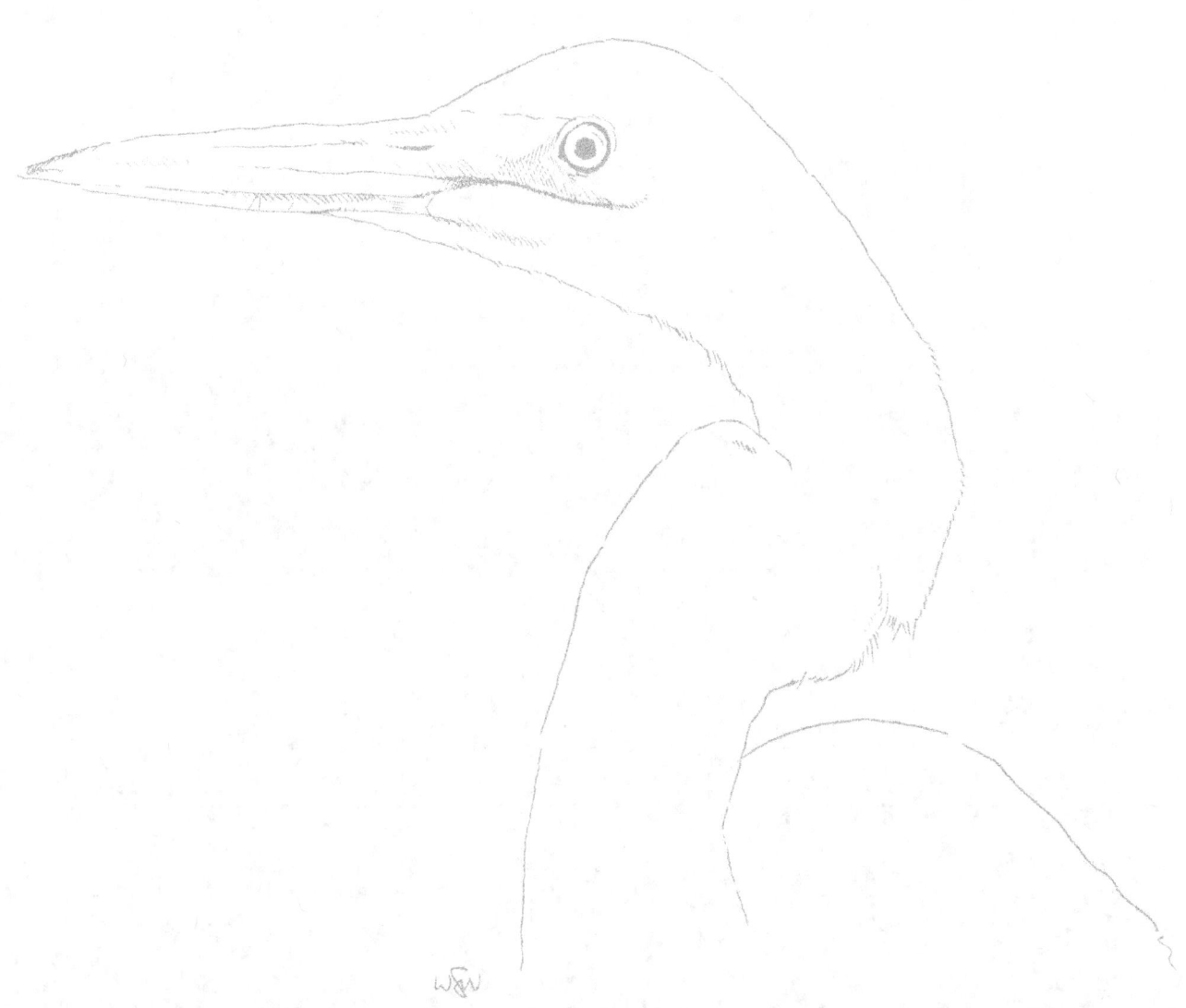

**White Egret**

Shadow

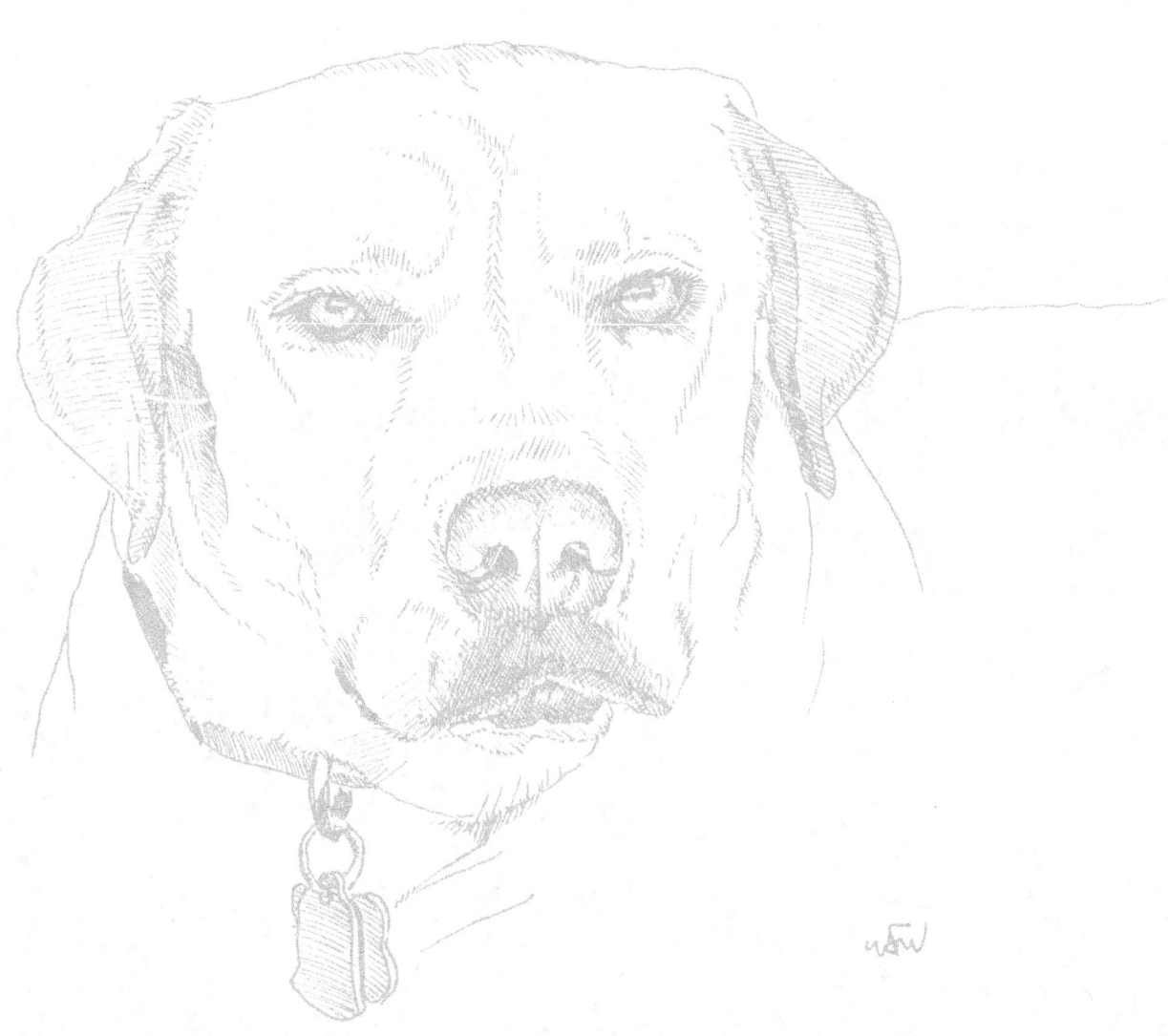

Winnie

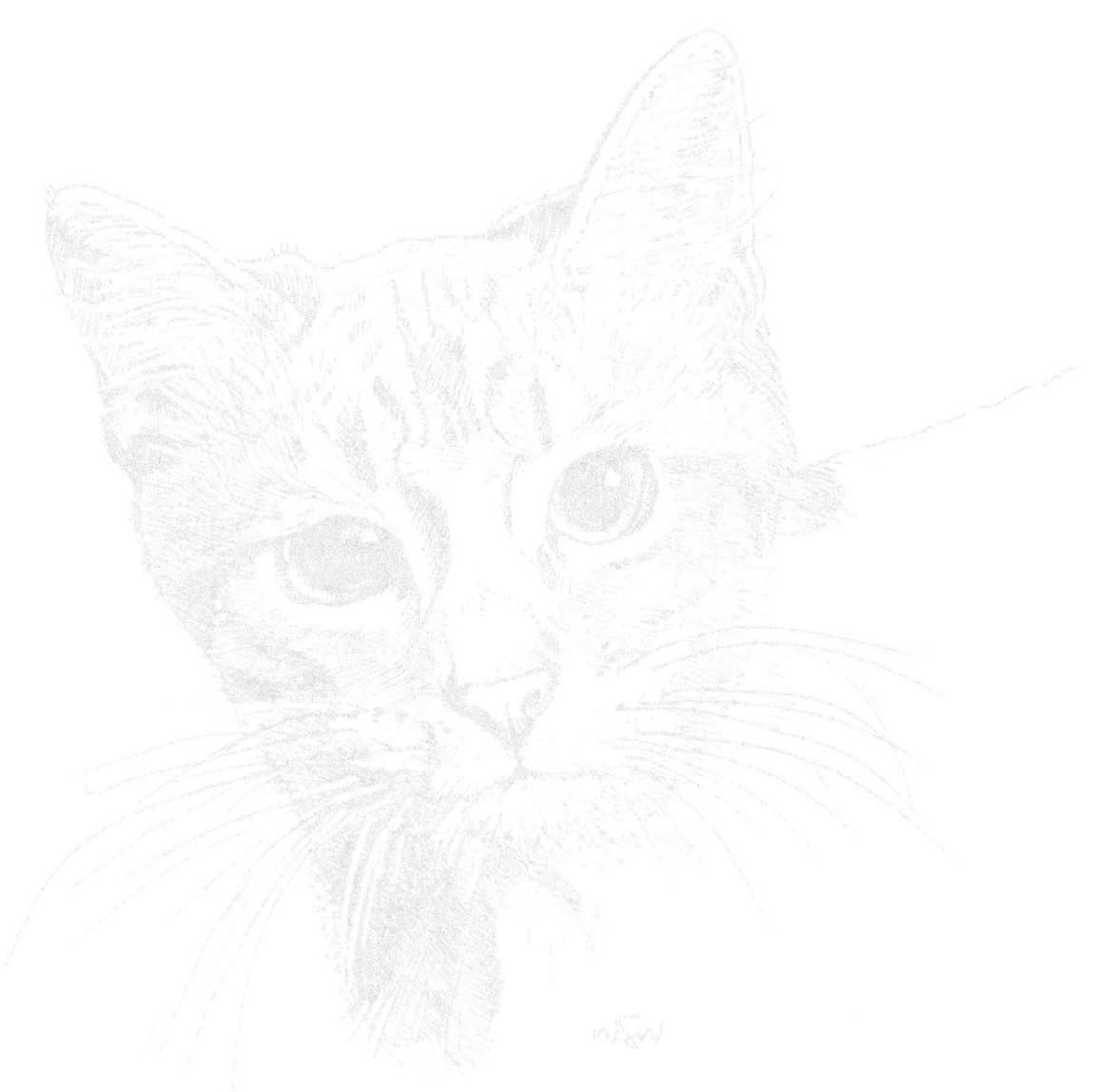

**Remy**

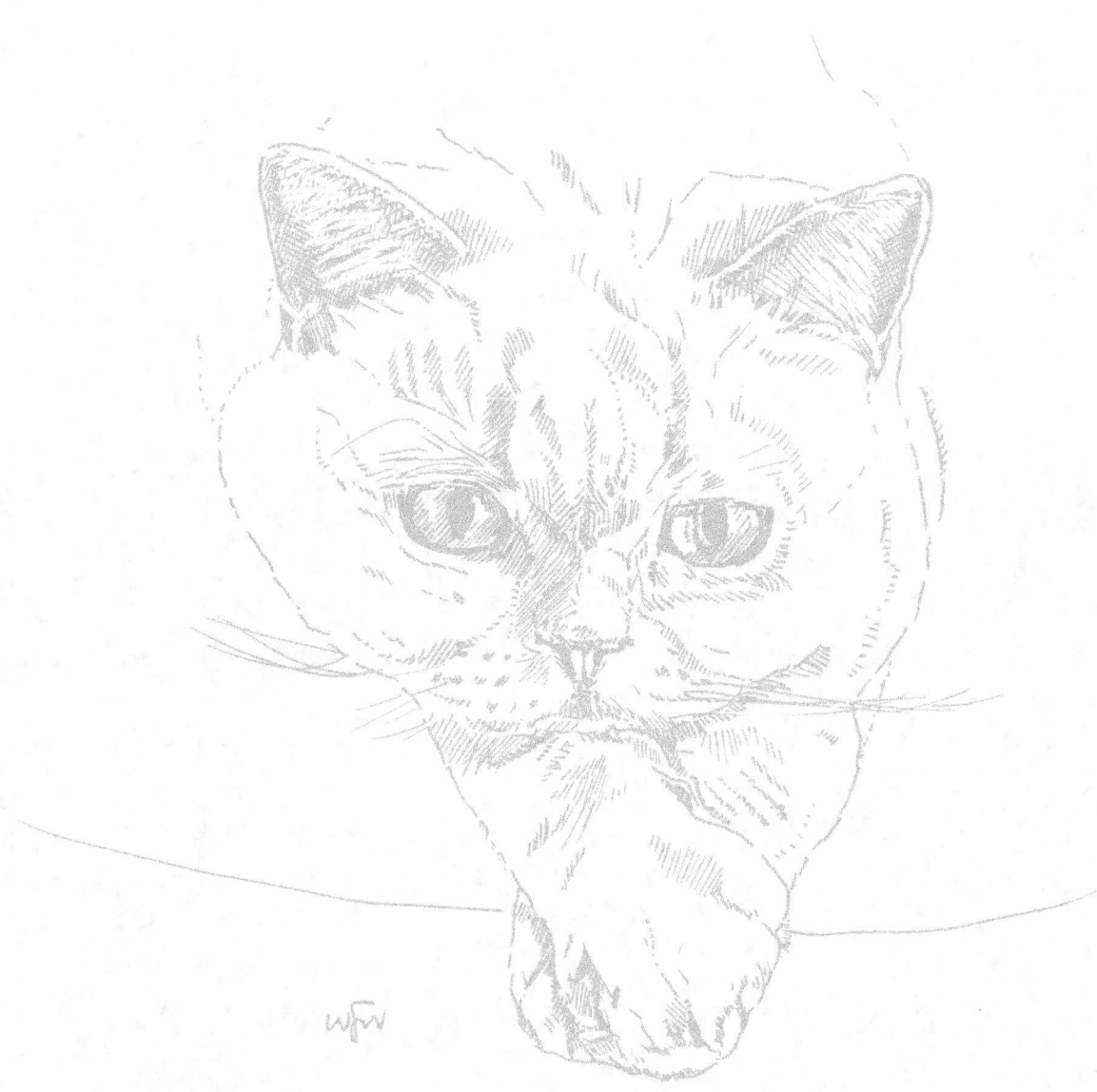

Lulu

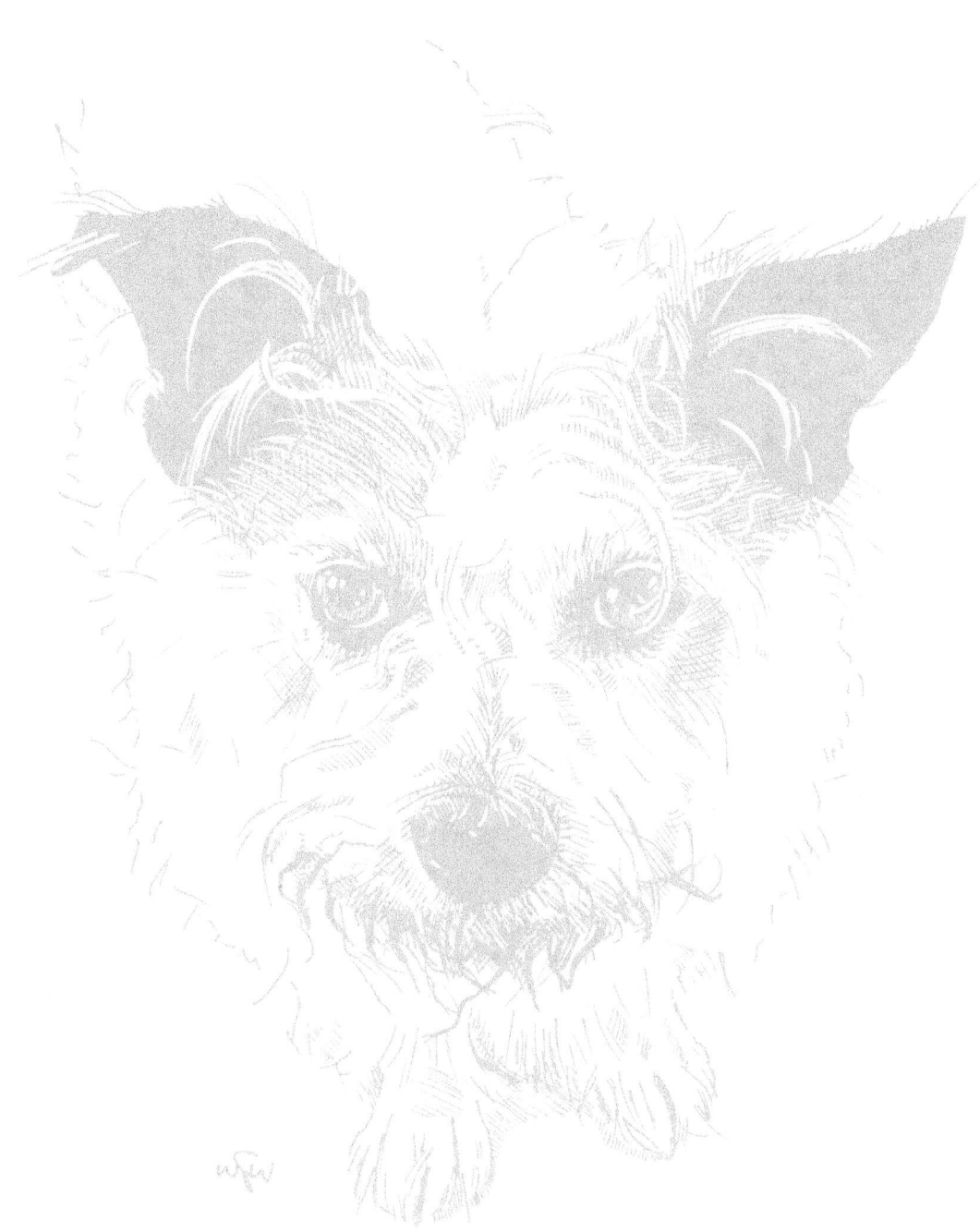

**Doodle**

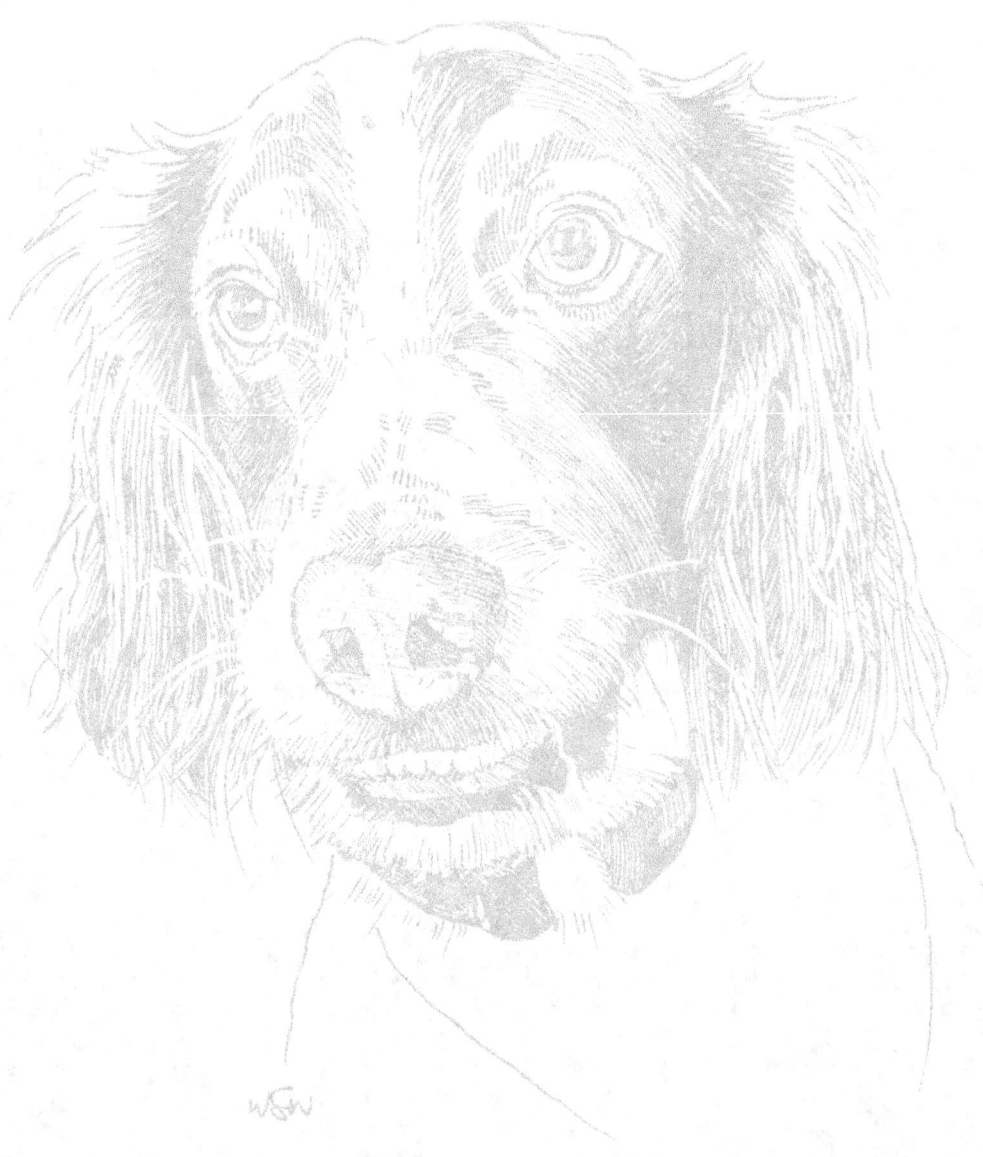

**Phineas**

**Fläck**

This coloring book is
a culmination of my
commissioned
pen & ink illustrations
from 2021-2024.

I rescued my very first
dog, Wrigley, when I
was 54 years old.

I was at the local SPCA
and I knew he was the
one. Especially when I
noticed his name was
already Wrigley!
As in Wrigley Field,
home of Chicago Cubs!

I can't imagine not
owning a dog ever
again! He's been my
best friend and
constant companion!

Let your colorful
imagination run wild! :)

www.ingramcontent.com/pod-product-compliance
Lightning Source LLC
Chambersburg PA
CBHW062234220526
45471CB00009B/3477